HISTORY HAS BEGUN

BRUNO MAÇÃES

History Has Begun

The Birth of a New America

HURST & COMPANY, LONDON

First published in the United Kingdom in 2020 by
C. Hurst & Co. (Publishers) Ltd.,
41 Great Russell Street, London, WC1B 3PL
© Bruno Maçães, 2020
All rights reserved.
Printed in Great Britain by Bell and Bain Ltd, Glasgow

The right of Bruno Maçães to be identified as the author of
this publication is asserted by him in accordance with the
Copyright, Designs and Patents Act, 1988.

A Cataloguing-in-Publication data record for this book
is available from the British Library.

ISBN: 9781787383012

This book is printed using paper from registered sustainable
and managed sources.

www.hurstpublishers.com

To Harvey Mansfield

"Is there anything more American than America?"

Bob Dylan

CONTENTS

PREFACE

We are unlearning old truths, a prelude to learning new ones. The values that have guided Western politics for decades or even centuries still seem true to most of us in the West, but they are true in a different way. They no longer seem inevitable. They may triumph in the end, but the playing field has been levelled. There are no impersonal forces pushing everyone towards the happy end of a society like those existing in North America or the European Union. In this new world, no triumph is ever definitive, which is to say that no triumph is ever a triumph.

The future is open. We are about to become the first human type to live entirely in history. Like human beings over the past three or four centuries, we live predominantly in the future and for the sake of the future. We are aware that nothing is permanent. Unlike our predecessors, we no longer believe that historical change has a meaning and direction. We are revolutionaries who have lost the faith in revolution.

For the moment, Western values seem in retreat. They are certainly not advancing, much less being irresistibly carried to every corner of the Earth. That we used to believe in their automatic expansion seems almost incredible now, but that does not mean that the situation has become hopeless. History does not take sides. It has not chosen liberal values, but neither has it chosen a new challenger. There is an implicit call here to join the battle, and that is the element in our predicament that is simultaneously unnerving and exciting.

So far the challenge to the old truths has come from the usual suspects. Almost as if the Soviet Union had never collapsed, the loudest voices in Russia continue to argue that what the West calls paradise is, when properly observed, the very idea of hell. It is a cry in the wilderness that never rises above a lonely cry because, when it comes to the decisive task of creation, Russia has failed or, at least, fallen short. Those who cannot live by the ruling values but are equally unable to produce new ones may justly be accused of having failed at the game.

China is a different case. This is a country that shows no evidence on converging with Western society on political and economic values, but whose ability to compete with the West seems undisputed. Whether the Chinese economy continues on the same path of fast growth or enters a period of malaise, few with knowledge of local realities will doubt its ability to master the sources of technological growth. It is precisely on this question that contemporary China has issued a serious challenge to liberal ideas. If China is able to demonstrate that Western society is not the only model capable of developing and controlling the key technologies of the future, global political competition will take place between different models and historical development will no longer follow a predetermined path. At that point, nothing will allow us to think that other major powers such as India cannot in the future look for their own political models in independence from existing alternatives.

I wrote about this possibility in previous books, before realizing that a much bigger question has been strangely neglected: might not the challenge to the ruling values come from inside the system rather than outside? I do not mean to say that a country such as the United States could enter a political crisis or even a process of institutional decline. That possibility is being discussed today. Many commentators see copious evidence of it and openly appeal to other societies to carry the liberal torch while Americans pass through their political distempers. But no political crisis, no matter how serious or prolonged, would provide much of a challenge to the dominant political values. In the absence of an alternative, even collapse would leave those values intact, waiting for a return or rebirth at the appropriate moment. Those who have spoken of liberal society as the final political model for mankind had their sights on the cunning of history, the influence of larger forces of which men and women may not be fully aware. There is room in this narrative for errors and catastrophes, crises and convulsions. The triumphal march of liberal democracy has been prodigal in setbacks.

For the United States to actively challenge the very values upon which it was founded, something else is needed. Not a process of collapse but an act of reinvention. I wrote in a previous book: "The United States may yet reveal itself as a shapeshifter. This prodigious child of the Enlightenment might not hesitate to shed Western, liberal principles if it becomes convinced that they have been refuted by time and experience. If ever the United States becomes convinced that the West belongs to the past, it could leave Europe living in that past, but it will not be inclined to remain there itself, especially if that would entail sacrificing the thing to which it is most addicted: global primacy. If the West ever falters, America will want to become less Western. As the fulcrum of world power moves away from the West, so will America."[1]

At first glance, it is possible to think that the country at the centre of the existing world order will also be the most conservative element in the system. It benefits from the system in greater measure and it likely has a sharper understanding of the organizing values. On the other hand, the centre of global power is free of the temptations to please and emulate. As for intuitive knowledge of the organizing values, might it not be the case that those who understand their appeal are also better positioned to discover their contradictions and to believe that they can overcome them?

In contrast to the generalized attack against liberalism being conducted in China, the reinvention happening in America is natural and spontaneous. It may be more difficult to perceive because it has evolved from within the liberal idea. Even when it departs from liberalism it does so more often than not in response to its inner limits and contradictions. If a new world is being born, it is doing so slowly and almost imperceptibly. In the game of civilization, much like in chess, one must move a piece at a time, keeping all others in place, until a new combination emerges.

The question with which this book opens thus finds a precise answer. The current moment in American history is both a moment of destruction and a moment of creation. It is a moment of destruction if one considers the values inherited from modern European culture and strongly affirmed during the first century of the republic, when the United States stood practically as a European colony. It is a moment of creation if one looks to more recent decades and attempts to project the transformations they announce into the immediate future. This book is an attempt to examine the subtle processes by which a new way of looking at the world slowly extends to every facet of individual and collective life. I opt to call this way of looking a civilization in order to express how different cultural, social and political elements form a coherent whole.

My second and comparatively more ambitious task is to attempt to decipher the logic of this new civilization. It is apparent that, in a way analogous to the core European civilization from which it descends, contemporary America is organized around a powerful ideal of individual freedom and creativity, but the way freedom is understood and expressed now differs rather dramatically on both sides of the Atlantic. The transatlantic world is not static but exists in time, from the origins of the modern sensibility and the birth of liberalism in Europe to a decidedly postmodern and postliberal experiment in America.

PREFACE

At a time when the nature of transatlantic relations is feverishly discussed—amid much anxiety about their vitality or even survival—we would do well to inject them with the pathos of history and change. E → A rather than E = A. Europe and America are not the same, they do not exist in a relation of identity, but they are deeply connected. They follow from each other and in the process issue a challenge to each other. America can thrive as an outgrowth of European civilization only to the extent that it offers a solution to its outstanding and deeply felt contradictions.

If it succeeds, American civilization will turn out to be something completely original. And this, as Keyserling would say, "is the best that could be said of it. What the world wants is the creation of new values. Repetition, even of the best, is contrary to the law of life ..."[2] The novelist and critic Waldo Frank argued in a book published in 1940 that just as a thousand years ago Europe knew a bloom from which ten centuries and America itself issued, so the United States of his time was experiencing "the chaos and the blindness, the dynamic impulse and the rightness of youth".[3] The collapse of the old world was approaching and America would finally have the chance to create a new one. Frank had the intuition of a beginning, but no sense yet of what this new world would look like. Though the epoch was American, the period was still European. It is up to us to provide a new picture. The reader may wish to turn to page 63 for the first reference to the secret of American civilization.

What is this American civilization about? What values does it hold? Conventional wisdom suggests that the United States has already reached its peak. But what if it is only now starting to forge its own path forward? What if American history is only just beginning? The pages that follow trace the story of the new America from its mysterious first apparitions to the present convulsions.

Angkor   *September 2019*

ONE

In 1836 the American landscape painter Thomas Cole completed an ambitious five-canvas historical allegory titled *The Course of Empire*. Today the series is something of an internet sensation, even if art critics will point out its imitative or naive elements. It is graphic, spectacular and pungent, and it carries a simple political message. Nations go through stages similar to an individual life. They are born, they grow and prosper, but inevitably decay sets in—or is it the pictures that got smaller? Death and destruction must follow.

The series begins with "The Savage State", a painting of nature untouched by human activity. A hunter clad in skins pursues a deer, while in the distance a cluster of primitive tents around a fire prefigures the city to be. The emergence of an agrarian civilization from this early tribe of hunters is the theme of the second painting, "The Arcadian or Pastoral State".

In "The Consummation of Empire", the third painting, we reach the apex of civilization. The scene looks garish and tasteless, but perhaps it is always like that with culture at its moment of fullest expression. Human figures fill every empty space and there is a whirl of excitement as an imperial procession crosses a bridge and leaves the scene on the left through a pink-and-golden arch. Opulence reigns, the architecture is excessive, and everything is finished and perfect—bright white marble covers every available surface. There is nothing left to achieve and one fears for civil peace when contemplating the excited mobs elbowing their way.

Nature follows the rhythms of empire. The first painting depicts the city at dawn, probably in spring, the second on a morning in early summer, the third at noon during a hot summer day. The fourth painting, "Destruction", is dark, dramatic, sublime. The scene is the sack and destruction of the city. An enemy fleet has sailed up the river, setting fire to the buildings and killing and raping the inhabitants. One has to conclude that their task was made easier by the state of luxury and laziness in which they found the city. There are contorted corpses everywhere and those trying to flee have improvised a wooden structure to cross the same bridge, now broken, which in the previous painting signified power and triumph. It is difficult to tell whether the dark clouds above result from the burning buildings or the storm raging beyond. Finally, in the last painting of the series, "Desolation", a long and final night has descended upon the city, where not a living soul appears and only the grandiose ruins of the past distinguish the scene from the beginning of the narrative. Nature is returning. New trees, bushes and ivy already cover many of the crumbling buildings, natural ruins drained of human energy. The lonely column in the foreground is a nesting place for birds.

The Course of Empire must be interpreted in the context of the social and political changes brought about by the presidency of Andrew Jackson, the seventh president of the United States, whose portrait now occupies a place of honour in Donald Trump's Oval Office. Jackson seemed to combine the worst tendencies of democracy and mob rule with imperious autocracy. To a certain patrician class of Americans, it must have seemed that the end was nigh. Suddenly the masses felt confident in their own power and an unprecedented expansion in credit led to rampant speculation and the threat of a financial collapse. What made conservatives uneasy about the new America was the erosion of moral, social and institutional restraints on individual self-interest. The bubble did eventually burst in 1837, the first of many large financial crises through which the United States climbed its way to the top of the global economy. A contemporary noted in his account of the crisis: "In 1835, the madness made further progress, and continued increasing up to 1836, in July, when it reached its height." Was America under Andrew Jackson reaching its final stage? To many it may have seemed that way, but we now know that it had barely reached the stage of an agrarian economy, while large swathes of future territory remained images of savage nature. And, in fact, for most Americans the paintings were supposed to represent the stories of ancient lands, not a lesson for their own time. Cole's contemporaries had stopped believing in history as a cycle of birth and death.

For many, the greatest threat to America was not the growth of democracy but the fact that it had yet to fulfil its promise. This was a narrative of progress and the hope in its future realization. They remembered Jefferson's forebodings about slavery: "And can the liberties of a nation be thought secure when we have removed their only firm basis, a conviction in the minds of the people that these liberties are the gift of God? That they are not to be violated but with his wrath? Indeed I tremble for my country when I reflect that God is just: that his justice cannot sleep for ever ..."

On the surface, it is Rome that *The Course of Empire* represents. The Roman Republic had been the model for the new American Republic and its dissolution appeared to the first two or three generations of Americans as the fate against which they had to guard themselves. Like the Romans, Americans had risen up and expelled their kings. They now lived in dread that the republic might succumb to internal corruption. In the image of the emperor sustained by a submissive and stupefied populace, Cole was evoking a common perception of Andrew Jackson. The narrative centre of the series evoked common feelings of republican danger fuelled by the loss of public virtue. But the classical world was also the source for a certain way of looking at history—where nations are caught in an incessant cycle of rise and fall—defended by seminal political thinkers such as Plutarch and Polybius.

Cole was obsessed by cyclical history and in his later years explicitly predicted the downfall of American democracy at the close of the twentieth century. In an unpublished science fiction tale, he describes a country whose population now numbers in the hundreds of millions. The landscape glitters with new cities and countless buildings, but material progress goes together with rampant corruption, irreligion and anarchy. "Human nature, and the historical laws that it generated, were everywhere the same; it was only a matter of time before the logic of these laws would catch up with, and triumph over, the exceptional conditions of American culture."[1]

Throughout his *Histories* the Greek historian Polybius tries to convey the lesson that when a nation departs from its founding principles, catastrophe is near at hand. When a state is growing in power, it needs to consider the feelings and thoughts of its neighbours. Pride and arrogance follow closely upon conquest, but they would never allow one to acquire empire and therefore should be considered a very inadequate tool for holding it.

Polybius frequently alludes to the fact that with expansion Rome started to suffer from corruption, indolence and luxury. Competition for wealth replaced competition for honour and distinction. When a state has warded off many serious threats, and has come to attain undisputed supremacy and sovereignty, lifestyles become more extravagant and rivalry over political positions and other such projects becomes fiercer than it should be. But was Polybius right? Rome survived for half a millennium beyond his death and many of its greatest achievements came in later centuries. This is especially true if we consider those achievements that seem to us inspired by an original and creative Roman character rather than Greek wisdom and knowledge: the genius of Caesar, the conquest of Egypt, the Pantheon, the philosophy of Marcus Aurelius, the poetry of Virgil or Ovid.

In the natural course of events, as Polybius sees it, the first political system to arise is monarchy, which is succeeded by kingship, where one person rules by consent, and then tyranny. "Aristocracy necessarily degenerates into oligarchy, and when the general populace gets impassioned enough to seek redress for the crimes committed by their leaders, democracy is born. And in due course of time, once democracy turns to violating and breaking the law, mob rule arises and completes the series." Everything naturally goes through successive phases of growth, prime and decline, and in every respect things are at their best during their prime. There is only one way to make the state last forever and that is to bundle together all the merits and distinctive characteristics of the best systems of government, maintained in a high degree of balance.

This is the natural course, but in the real world states do not simply decay and restart. They are conquered if too weak or if more powerful rivals grow in their neighborhood. Competition and not natural decay is the main reason to build a balanced political system. In that case, when a general threat from abroad forces citizens and classes to cooperate and collaborate, the state gains extraordinary abilities: everyone works together in their public and private capacities to complete the task at hand; there is no contingency that it is incapable of meeting. "This gives the Roman state its characteristic feature: it is irresistible, and achieves every goal it sets itself." While in Carthage the common people had by then become the dominant political force, in Rome this was still the Senate. Since policy was decided in Carthage by the masses and in Rome by the best men, Roman policies would prevail.

Polybius, a Greek exile and captive, is not in a position to claim that no state is immortal, but he has no illusions about that. He quotes the words of Scipio Aemilianus after the consul succeeded in finally entering Carthage and destroying the city, Rome's old rival for control of the Mediterranean. Scipio looked upon the ruins and reflected that all cities and nations, like human beings, must one day meet their doom. All the empires of Media, Persia, Macedonia, so brilliant in their time, had come to an end. Why should any later exemplar have a different fate? Old verses from Homer escaped his lips: "A day will come when sacred Troy shall perish." When Polybius asked him what he meant by the verses, "they say that without any attempt at concealment he named his own country, for which he feared when he reflected on the fate of all things human."[2] At the very moment of triumph—and disaster for his fiercest enemy—the young Roman statesman understood that Rome too would one day lie in ruins.

In a book published in 2010, the legal scholar Bruce Ackerman argued against what he still saw as America's constitutional triumphalism. He regarded it as a sign of terminal decline. In the past Americans were very reluctant to consider their constitutional system as perfect. They were too busy improving it. Ackerman worried that once triumphalism became dominant, the energy that had kept the American experiment going would disappear as well. Much of his analysis comes close to the way of thinking of classical historians such as Polybius. Every republic starts with a given capital of vitality. It will use it to face and overcome the crises that are a necessary part of political life, but in time that capital will be depleted. Or to describe the dialectic in a different way, each successful attempt to solve a political or constitutional problem will create a new problem which will need to be solved in turn. And since many solutions do not even manage to address the underlying issue, problems keep multiplying and the system keeps getting weaker when it should in fact need greater and greater resources.

Ackerman does not blame the original system for the great constitutional crisis he sees coming. That system had at least been tested. It overcame many dangerous moments for the constitution and the republic. But the current political and constitutional system of the United States is almost unrecognizable. It was born of the very process by which the American republic faced the challenges of the last two centuries. Ominously, every dangerous pathology Ackerman is able to find turns out to be relatively recent and his fear is that we are approaching the moment when they will start to interact with each other, when all the pieces of a picture of decline—the Course of Empire—have been put in place.[3]

What does he predict, then? Firstly, that the presidential nomination system will produce an increasing number of outsiders elected because they have mobilized public opinion around extreme and unconventional programmes. Secondly, presidents will increasingly rely on political polarization with extreme messages tailored to different micro-publics. Thirdly, they will rely on super-loyalists more than on the public bureaucracy and they will look for new ways to use their executive powers over the military. Fourthly, they will appeal to national emergencies and specific mandates from the public to override constitutional procedures. Ackerman concludes that "these are the dynamics for the decline and fall of the American Republic."[4]

Many of these points seem remarkably prescient—both Obama and Trump have helped bring those possibilities closer to reality—but on one thing at least Ackerman turned out to be wrong. He finished his book with the renewed concern that Americans had become too triumphant: the recognition that the American constitutional tradition is in serious trouble "is entirely lacking at present. If anything, Americans are more prone to celebrate the eternal wisdom of the Founding Fathers than they were a generation ago."[5] This may or may not have been true a decade ago, but since then we have entered a new period where the collective mood has embraced the narrative of decline, where the darkest gloom has descended upon Washington, and where Americans have become fixated on images of dictators, civil war and the ruins of empire. Popular novels such as *Tropic of Kansas* and *American War* depict a plausible future where the United States has collapsed: a fascist president has been elected, killer drones patrol the skies, football stadiums have been turned into prisons, a second Civil War has broken out, Texas is invaded by Mexico, and guerrillas ravage the land.

Many contemporary commentators argue that American elites now regard their own country as spoils to be fought over. Currents over the past four decades express the relentless pursuit of private interest at the expense of the common good, even when that pursuit may bring about the final collapse of the system. Privatization, deregulation, the rise of finance—these are contemporary versions of the old dialectic of decline. Private groups try to grab a larger share of wealth and power and others sense that they too must make their move while there is still a healthy political and economic core to prey on. The gulf between economic and intellectual elites and the rest of the people seems larger than ever before. Any sense of the common good disappears from view as opposing classes are pitched against each other. In Washington, Democrats and Republicans are no longer capable of reaching compromises on important policies and often regard winning their disputes as the only thing that matters.

The writer David Klion no longer sees a standing polity in America. He speaks instead of a global platform or global market for influence and corruption, "in which outside powers can purchase influence, shape political outcomes, and play factions against each other in the service of their own competing agendas."[6] It is a fate common to many great empires of the past, rendered apart by external powers and agents of influence. Many countries of course spend large fortunes trying to lobby lawmakers in Washington. Others appeal to sentiment or acquire the services of communications companies expert at mobilizing public opinion. Is there anything left or has the United States become an arena where others pursue their interests? And of course many of the biggest companies in America are multinational, with headquarters in major cities around the world and executives whose loyalties lie much more obviously with their international counterparts than with most Americans. What we are witnessing, Klion concludes, is not a withdrawal from empire, but a decadent collapse recognizable to any student of Rome or Constantinople. An old tale of decline and fall.

Jeet Heer wonders whether, as a porn star sues President Donald Trump and the White House is drained of everyone but his family, America might not be entering into a period of decadence that rivals Imperial Rome in luridness.[7] *New Yorker* editor David Remnick predicted that future scholars will sift through contemporary tweets the way we now read Suetonius, "to understand how an unhinged emperor can make a mockery of republican institutions, undo the collective nervous system of a country, and degrade the whole of public life."[8] Bill Kristol tweeted that he was impressed by the speed at which the United States is recapitulating the decline and fall of Rome: "What took Rome centuries we are achieving in months." Tom Holland reflects on yet another historical parallel. Cassius, the assassin of Julius Caesar, was saluted by Brutus, his fellow conspirator, as the last of the Romans. "It was in a similar spirit that mourners gathered in September 2018 to bid farewell to John McCain, a man whose record as a soldier and a senator had an authentically Roman timbre."[9]

But Trump is only a small part of the narrative of decline. Tyler Cowen provides a fuller picture of all the ways American life is reaching a breaking point, at a moment when disaggregating forces are getting stronger. Productivity growth has been slowing down and, with current debt levels so high, America will have to raise taxes or cut public expenditure. To fund the budget shortfall, future administrations will be forced to cut back on infrastructure and the military. China and Russia will have an easier time exercising control over their regions and American influence will disappear from many parts of the world. Drug overdoses and addiction will grow exponentially as new and more powerful substances are developed. Public surveillance will reach unthinkable levels. The spread of killer drones may be contained, perhaps, by filling the skies with police drones. Technology will make daily life in China and the United States increasingly indistinguishable. And there is little to do because all these developments follow powerful economic and social forces, quite independently of who actually sits in the Oval Office.[10]

What was responsible for all this was not Trump, although he may have made the whole process much more vivid and personal. It was the wars in Afghanistan and Iraq, which were meant to bring the American way of life into the farthest corners of the world—twenty years later, after heavy losses in treasury and lives, the United States is getting ready to hand Afghanistan back to the Taliban. It was Katrina and other natural disasters, which for long periods made the United States look like a failed state. It was the global financial crisis, from which vast segments of the country never really recovered, and the living contradiction between the sense of national emergency it awakened and the complacency with which the system responsible for the crisis has been left more or less intact. It was the crumbling or outdated infrastructure, which went in half a century from awing foreign visitors to making them wonder if they had in fact landed in the right country. Take the case of New York City: incredible as it may sound, no major new piece of public infrastructure has been built within the five boroughs of the city since the opening of the Verrazzano bridge connecting Brooklyn to Staten Island. When Trump arrived on the scene and said that America was no longer great but needed, once again, to be made great, people knew what he was talking about

The recent texts I have referred to above ask the very same question Thomas Cole was interested in. Where in the cycle of birth and death do we place contemporary America? Is it still in the state of consummation, a country at the height of its powers? Or has it passed to the state of destruction, rife with internal conflict and on the verge of institutional collapse? Perhaps it lies somewhere in-between the two; after all, one of the most important elements in any theory of cycles is the interstitial space between the different states. Or, then, as I plan to argue in this book, perhaps the United States is only just entering its highest period, where its individual possibilities will be realized. Yes, that is possible too. Civilizations in the past were always measured in much longer periods than the metrics we like to use for America. Remember that the pyramids were built near the beginning of Egyptian civilization and more than 2,000 years before its conventionally accepted end.

Part of the problem is that we are no longer sure how to think about historical change. I noted above that Cole was unusual among his contemporaries in still subscribing to a deeply conservative philosophy of history according to which human societies follow natural cycles of birth and destruction. That view was replaced by the belief in endless progress towards a steady state of development. The theory of cycles failed to distinguish between the natural and the human worlds. As human beings increased their ability to master nature, it was thought that they could use their abilities to build new societies increasingly free from want and conflict. The replacement of religious superstition with modern science would ensure that new and better solutions could be found for all the problems of government. The American Constitution itself was perceived in this way, an instance of political technology more modern and efficient than every available alternative. Ultimately, in the absence of a natural or divine authority, history depends on us, and it may be presumed that, if made aware of the fact, human beings will take full advantage of an open future. One might even postulate, as Marx did, that every question humankind is able to pose is by definition a question it is able to solve.

Ironically, it seems that philosophies of history more than history itself must follow a hard cycle of rise and fall. We no longer believe in progress, and not only because the twentieth century has given us more reason to believe in barbarism and destruction. For us, progress is a limiting idea which, having introduced us to the possibility of an open future, left it very much closed. The future is the true focus of history.

The narrative of progress, the belief in history as improvement, and the hope in a rational society as the final outcome of historical change—these are ideas developed within a particular life form. For people living elsewhere or for other periods in history, progress and change would have very different meanings. The constellation of values according to which life is interpreted would be different and the struggles to realize these values would in many cases be unrecognizable. What from the point of view of progressive thought looks like a constricted path is in fact empty space where infinite lines may be drawn and movement has no preordered direction or even necessity. This is a world full of losses, reversions, false starts, catastrophes. There is never a path, but when many people walk on it, the path comes into existence.

ONE

The main question for us is no longer where to place America on the path of modern progress—the counterpart, as many have argued, of supernatural creation—but to discover what is this America we are considering and to answer that question in the framework of empty historical space, an empty canvas of creation, where everything or almost everything is prima facie possible.

Oswald Spengler famously argued that, just as every organism has a form, rhythm and duration proper to the species, so human history follows the same law. The difference is that we are prone, in what concerns the survival of our own species, to disregard natural limits and imagine a universal history of humankind organized according to successive stages of development or growth. Our time, hitherto looked on as the highest point of an ascending straight line, is in reality a stage of life which may be observed in every culture that has ripened to its limit. Words may well fail us, but cool reflection teaches that to birth belongs death; to youth, age; to life generally, its form and its allotted span. Time is a river, a violent current of events, glimpsed once and already carried past us, and another follows and is gone.

There is no linear history but the drama of a number of main cultures. The challenge is to draw their identifying traits, a task at which Spengler is, despite himself, very perfunctory. Each culture has its own, novel possibilities. Birth, growth, strength, decline, and death. And then rebirth, but on what Spengler calls a special type of growth and decline, "a picture of endless formations and transformations, of the marvellous waxing and waning of organic forms."[11]

If every culture has a lifespan and a biography, what can one say of the state of Western Europe and America in the last century or two? Interestingly, in the original edition of his magnum opus Spengler spoke rather determinedly of the Western European as the ruling culture of his time, but eventually he forced himself to accept political realities and later editions started to speak of "the only Culture of our time and on our planet which is actually in the phase of fulfillment—the West European-American."[12]

Since every culture goes through its own phases of birth, growth and decline, Spengler is naturally attracted to the spirit of analogy—he is to a great extent known for the uses he makes of "symmetry of structure" or the "method of comparative morphology in world history". The Great War—the great crisis of our civilization—corresponded for him to the transition from Greece to Rome in classical culture. The analogy is meant to instruct us in the life phases of different cultures. When it comes to their content, they have nothing in common and the modern historian simply deludes himself if he thinks that "republic", "democracy" or "property" meant the same thing for the Greeks as they do for us. Formally, however, they follow similar rhythms of growth and decline.

Now, the lifespan of classical culture is for Spengler marked by a crucial transition from Greeks to Romans, a transition in which the end of classical culture is already prefigured. Of the Romans he writes: "Unspiritual, unphilosophical, devoid of art, clannish to the point of brutality, aiming relentlessly at tangible successes, they stand between the Hellenic Culture and nothingness."[13]

There is an important question which Spengler notably fails to raise, at least explicitly. If the Romans represent the final stage in the history of classical culture, who are the modern Romans, which country is fated to take Western culture to its final denouement and collapse? Sometimes he seems to suggest America will take up the role. He comments, for example, that "in depopulated Athens, which lived on visitors and on the bounty of rich foreigners, the mob of parvenu tourists from Rome gaped at the works of the Periclean age with as little understanding as the American globetrotter in the Sistine Chapel at those of Michelangelo."[14] But elsewhere it is the Germany of his time that is supposed to lead us to the end in a vortex of communal spirit, high finance and worldwide militarism. Rome, with its rigorous realism, uninspired, barbaric, disciplined, practical and Protestant was Prussian, and Prussia was Roman.

Were he writing today, Spengler would probably argue that the last nation of the West turned out to be the United States, an outpost nation, far from Europe but thoroughly imbued with European culture. The symmetry with Rome appealed to his contemporaries. In 1918 Max Weber advised friends to accept than an American empire was as inevitable as that of Rome in antiquity after the Punic Wars, adding that he hoped that world empire would not be shared with Russia, "since the Russian danger has been averted only for now, not forever."[15] Just like Rome, America was the cultural offshoot of an older culture, established on its periphery and meant to assume the mantle of leadership in the very process of cultural expansion.[16] Harold Macmillan, later the British prime minister, would take the thought to its logical conclusion, explaining to a confidant during the critical moments of World War Two: "We are Greeks in this American empire, you will find the Americans much as the Greeks found the Romans—great big vulgar, bustling people, more vigorous than we are and also more idle, with more unspoiled virtues, but also more corrupt."[17]

There is a problem with this thesis. While Rome acquired its superpower status in a deadly struggle against Carthage, America did so in a long and protracted struggle against Europe, its core civilization. What I have in mind is less the War of Independence against England, relevant as that undoubtedly is, than the conflicts of the twentieth century, where the United States was not trying to salvage Europe from its dark nemesis—could one really argue that the Germany of Goethe and Beethoven was not European?—but saving the world from the inner demons of European culture. Spengler remarks in *Prussianism and Socialism* that the Americans, this new people, arose apart from the maternal soil of Western European culture, and thus lacked the inner soul of the culture. To be sure, "it retained certain traces of noble blood and the concomitant virtues of vigour and industriousness, but was without roots and therefore without a future."

Already on the eve of entering the Great War, a psychological break had taken place. American public opinion saw that in the United States many different nations could live together—French, Germans, Austrians, Russians and Englishmen worked together in friendly fashion—whereas in the "torrid crater of European hatreds it seemed as though the world had gone back centuries." The shock of the shift in view was no less profound because it was largely subconscious.[18] After Auschwitz it became conscious.

There are two ways of regarding the question of America. For great thinkers of civilization such as Spengler or Toynbee—writing in the first decades of the twentieth century—America must have seemed like a gigantic replica of Europe, a replica that by virtue of its very gigantism exposed the internal processes of excess and decline that they had discovered in Europe. Fundamental differences of culture and feeling—those they failed to perceive.

For us, a century later, the question takes a different form. If we return to Spengler and Toynbee it is to understand what comes after the West. More aware of the distinctiveness of American society than they could ever be, we want to know whether the dynamism of the United States in the twentieth century might not prefigure something new and whether the current turmoil could in fact be better interpreted as the birth pangs of a new culture instead of—much as Spengler and Toynbee dismissed the European culture of their time—the death throes of an aged civilization.

There were facts and there are facts militating against the interpretation of America as part of modern Western society.

Firstly, as already noted, the United States affirmed its global primacy much more often against Europe than with it. This fact is often obscured and may seem counterintuitive to some; we shall have to take it up again later in this book. Secondly, America was always conscious that it descended from many different nations or civilizations, the new country was a crossing of many strains of culture and history. Keyserling wrote: "The American presents a curious picture: a European with the manners of a negro and the soul of an Indian."[19] More soberly, Max Lerner spoke of four great migration families that in turn moved to the American continent. Only one was European. There were the American Indians. Their complex myths and cosmologies, their kinship systems, their language and dances, all this rich culture may have been violently destroyed, but they still left their mark on the American mind, if only as the ghost of an alternative history, the road not taken. There were also the slaves brought from Africa. As Lerner puts it, "in the contact of European and African cultures in America something striking was bound to happen to the new amalgam. The quality of American music, dance, literature, theater, religion, today is evidence that it did."[20] There was the final polyglot mass of migrants: Russians, Jews, Mexicans, Latin Americans and then Chinese, Japanese, Filipinos. For contemporary Americans, recognition of this multiple heritage has become a moral duty, one pushing it away from Europe.

More generally, the notion that the most powerful country on Earth would forever remain a tributary to ideas and feelings developed elsewhere has struck many as implausible. It does strike me as implausible, even before adding to it another point of perhaps even greater significance. The fact is that the status of Western society has changed in recent decades. Two centuries ago the country of Jefferson and Washington knew that the world was ruled by Europe and according to European ideas, and quickly made them its own. Today the proposition that the whole planet is on course to embrace Western civilization is no longer credible. One would expect the only global superpower to acquire a level of distance from those ideas or, at least, to re-examine them in full and even contemplate how they can be revised and improved.

If we consider the fractious nature of the contemporary American debate on foreign policy, it is apparent that a number of axioms are being questioned with increasing vigour. Does the liberal world order appeal equally to different regions of the world? Are different political traditions moving towards a liberal consensus, even if haltingly? Is there an intimate connection between democracy and human rights, on the one hand, and economic dynamism and power, on the other? Does the world need and welcome American leadership? Does globalization suit American interests, promoting prosperity and security for all Americans? Does globalization encourage cooperation between different countries or, on the contrary, does it intensify competition and rivalry? Compared to Europe, the United States does have the resources to apply the modern principle of reform to the very organizing principles of American society. It remains to be seen if this change can be felt as a change for the better rather than a surrender to the outside.

The present challenge to Western society comes of course from Asia, where we shall soon find four of the five largest economies in the world. The success of the Chinese economy has been built on political principles far removed from the Western liberal tradition, and no real chance of ultimate convergence is currently being contemplated. If anything, we may witness the attempt to follow China in adopting a number of ideas that until recently have been anathema in the West. If the Chinese succeed in leading the revolutionary advancement in new technologies such as robotics and artificial intelligence, this process may accelerate.

One scenario therefore would be this: just as America received the influx of European ideas and population in the centuries just before and after its political constitution, it could now receive a similar influx across the Pacific and end up as a hybrid Eurasian culture, as perhaps befits a land whose native culture and way of life were systematically uprooted and eradicated. There might be some early evidence for this scenario in the fact that Asians are projected to become the largest share of the immigrant population of the United States by the middle of the century, but for my part I remain highly sceptical that a second colonization of North America is possible, let alone probable. In this book I defend a second future scenario: the development of a new, indigenous American society, separate from modern Western civilization, rooted in new feelings and thoughts. What then is the American, this new man?

When Toynbee tries to delimit the extension of Western culture or society in time, he starts by noting that while we cannot see into the future—and ignorance of how the West will end greatly restricts our ability to understand its full nature—it is nonetheless possible to explore the time extension of Western society in the direction of its origins. It immediately seems obvious to him that civilizations are not born out of nothing, and to that rule the West must equally subscribe. To understand the West's origins is to understand its relation to the Hellenic society out of which it emerges. The Roman Empire succeeded in incorporating the whole of Hellenic society into a single political unit at the very moment when this society was reaching its end, a phase when it was no longer creative and seemed in patent decline. The Roman Empire's fall was followed by a kind of interregnum, during which a new beginning was quietly being prepared. Predictably, it is not at the centre—where the old values retained their hold—that one could find the cradle of our own Western society. On the social plane, it was the excluded, the proletariat as Toynbee calls them, who were now developing new images and thinking of new values. The Christian Church was growing from within the Empire just as it disintegrated, slowly assimilating its ambitions and preparing to take its place. While they occupied the same space, the Empire was a living corpse, while the Church was full of vitality. As Toynbee puts it, the interregnum gave the Church the opportunity to perform an "act of creation". The Church played the part of a chrysalis out of which emerged in the fullness of time modern Western society, with all its characteristic institutions of representative government, industrial development, the belief in the dignity and duty of labour with its distant Cistercian echoes, the balance of power between temporal and spiritual power.[21]

Geographically, the new society established itself on the periphery. The cradle from which our Western society has developed—a belt stretching from Rome to Aachen and across the Channel to the Roman Wall—coincided with part of the border of the Roman Empire. As Toynbee writes, during the interregnum which preceded the emergence of our Western world, "a rib was taken from the side of the older society and was fashioned into the backbone of a new creature of the same species."[22] The forced migration of Oriental labour to the western parts of the Roman Empire after the Punic Wars had brought with it new religious beliefs promising salvation to populations already despairing of the future. The Church, expanding towards the western frontier, was met by the opposite expansion of Germans, Slavs and Huns from the forests and steppes beyond, and the pincer movement—the union of the internal and external proletariats—gave birth to a new society.[23] As for the logic of geographic displacement, it is of course reminiscent of the American epic: a society is built on the fringes of the European world, but in time becomes a new centre. A rib was taken from the side of modern European society and ... The only question is whether it has become the new centre of the old culture or a new centre of a new culture.

The continuity in the history of a single society resembles the succession of experiences in the life of a single person. The continuity between successive and directly related societies—such as that between the classical and Western cultural universes— resembles the relations between parent and child. If we take the analogy further, it will become apparent that the birth of a new culture, with its dramatic tones, remains a period when the child is dominated by the parental environment and, consciously or unconsciously, imitates parental feelings and thoughts. The genuine beginning, the moment of maturity and independence, will come later and must be much less dramatic and more difficult to isolate. The meaning of the analogy seems clear and can be readily applied to the American experiment.

In a speech in Springfield in January 1838, Lincoln speaks of the founding generation in America as a race of immortals. Those coming after on the living stage are no more than the legal heirs, mere continuators or imitators, of a previous and original feat. George Washington had a subtler view of the matter. In 1793 he explained that Americans enjoyed the great advantage of being able to choose their form of government at a time when the rights of mankind were better understood and more clearly explained than at any previous period. The treasures of knowledge, acquired through the work of philosophers and statesmen over many years, were ready to be used and their accumulated wisdom could be put to work in the establishment of new forms of government. It should not surprise us that the American founding constitutes a clear and even dramatic beginning. It was guided by ideas that were fully developed and according to which events could be readily and easily interpreted. By contrast, the creation of modern Europe is lost in an uncertain past because the principles being established were so radically new that they could not be adequately perceived and interpreted. In his *History of the American Revolution*, published in 1789, David Ramsay compares the free governments of antiquity or the modern limited governments in Europe with the constitution created in America. The difference? The former were arranged by accident while in the latter the human species had for the first time the chance to decide under which kind of government it wanted to live. In the United States the beginning took place within a stable framework of accepted principles. And thus, paradoxically, it could be perceived as a beginning. Jefferson avowed that in the Declaration of Independence he had avoided all originality and only sought to "place before mankind the common sense of the subject."

Suppose you wanted to build a system of government on the best political principles. There would be two main difficulties. Firstly, as David Hume argued, it is not with forms of government as with other inventions. Experts may decide what is the best shape for a sailing ship, and in time all manufacturers will be forced to adopt it, if only to compete against the early adopters. But an established government has many advantages, prominently among them that of being accepted and understood by the ruled. Bring it down in order to build a better system, and you may end up with chaos rather than perfection, a lesson painfully learned by political projectors from the French Revolution to the Iraq War. Hume asks: "As one form of government must be allowed more perfect than another, independent of the manners and humours of particular men; why may we not enquire what is the most perfect of all, though the common botched and inaccurate governments seem to serve the purposes of society, and though it be not so easy to establish a new system of government, as to build a vessel upon a new construction?"[24] His answer is that one may attempt it through "gentle alterations and innovations" or then, a more radical method, "by the combination of men to form a new one, in some distant part of the world." The latter idea was especially tempting and it certainly appealed to those such as Jefferson, Madison or Hamilton who played a role in the founding of the American regime and who happened to be living in some distant part of the world. It was then incorporated into every theory of the American experiment, starting with Tocqueville, who saw it as the conclusion and perfection of the European political and intellectual tradition.

The second difficulty with this kind of political utopianism is that it is always much more decisively turned towards the past than towards the future. The attempt to create an ideal society presupposes that one has long familiarity with its inspiring principles and values. Such an attempt is a late progeny of every process of cultural development and may even be a symbol of its exhaustion. A living culture, still occupied with the practical and intellectual task of transforming the world, has no clear awareness of the forces inspiring it. Every deliberate act of political creation is mere repetition and every genuine act of creation is a slow, dark, mysterious and troubled struggle. The first American founding is a creature of the former type. This book is a study of the second founding, belonging to the latter. By comparison, the first founding was nothing.

Among the founding generation, it was Hamilton who took a significant further step. In a stirring text, he noted a fact, perhaps obvious, but of great importance: Europe and America belonged to two different hemispheres and, as a result, the proposition that the United States would eventually find a place within the European system of states defied the rules of political geography. Hamilton sees the new republic as an external actor, a different system, hoping "to become the arbiter of Europe in America, and to be able to incline the balance of European competitions in this part of the world as our interest may dictate." He imagines an age of unparalleled growth for America and argues that it can only happen against and at the expense of Europe. His message is one of gradual separation and sovereignty. With wisdom, the United States "might make herself the admiration and envy of the world." Hamilton imagines a time when Europe will no longer control the rest of the globe: "The world may politically, as well as geographically, be divided into four parts, each having a distinct set of interests. Unhappily for the other three, Europe, by her arms and by her negotiations, by force and by fraud, has, in different degrees, extended her dominion over them all. Africa, Asia, and America have successively felt her domination. The superiority she has long maintained has tempted her to plume herself as the Mistress of the World, and to consider the rest of mankind as created for her benefit."[25] He prophesies: "Let the thirteen States, bound together in a strict and indissoluble Union, concur in erecting one great American system, superior to the control of all transatlantic force or influence, and able to dictate the terms of the connection between the old and the new world!"

Yes, this may well be—it almost certainly is—meant as political propaganda. Hamilton needed to bridge divisions between the American states and inspire them with the image of a great rival and a commensurably great task for the united republic. Anything less than that might be insufficient to show the necessity of a federation. But that makes it even more interesting that Europe should be picked as the foil. Hamilton reads like the original critic of Western hegemony, and the new American republic is introduced as a project to overturn it.

TWO

The hold of the past over the American mind is the main road-block in the way of a genuine national rebirth. Its grip has been built over many layers. Political actions take a certain direction, feelings and perceptions give them meaning, but what protects those actions from radical change is the system of ideas. The layer of theory and reflection is the hardest to break because it is often taken as a natural and inevitable part of the world's fabric.[1] We must not ignore it. The meaning of America is present as much in the great books written about the American experiment as in the most practical elements of its politics and economic life. The image of America as a representative of European civilization was built over two centuries by thinkers and writers for whom no alternative was yet conceivable or for whom a transatlantic community offered a distinct promise of happiness. Many of these writers were European, others were American.

Even someone such as Max Lerner, who tried to investigate the distinctive traits of an American civilization and was perhaps the first to devote serious effort to the task, ended up arguing that the American was the "archetypal man of the West". In his influential 1957 book *America as a Civilization* he describes the American character as a concentrated embodiment of the European dream of power and emancipation, a type invented in Europe after the Renaissance and the Reformation: mobile, restless, cosmopolitan, searching for new experiences, breaking taboos, building machines and machines that run machines. After admitting that America must be integrated into broader Western patterns—that it is at most a more extreme version of modern European history—he is forced to confess his failure. It was perhaps too early. Someone else would have to find the "key that unlocks all doors", the "secret of American civilization".[2]

Responding to the playwright Luigi Pirandello, who had argued that a new American civilization was swamping Europe, the Marxist Antonio Gramsci clarified matters: there was no new civilization in America because "all they do in America is to remasticate the old European culture." It was entirely possible, he conceded, that the United States, through the sheer weight of its economic superpower, would compel Europe to change its traditional social and economic structures. But then "this would have happened anyway, though only slowly." For Gramsci, what those around him called Americanism was an "organic extension and intensification of European civilization, which has simply acquired a new coating in the American climate." The difference between America and Europe was not one of nature but of degree. At the time he was writing—in 1934—Berlin might appear more American than Paris, but that was not because Berlin had been conquered while Paris resisted. The reason was that Germany had been through a series of violent crises opening the way for new productive methods and social relations.[3]

Wealth and power will not be enough to provide Americans with a new understanding of their place in the history of civilization. Only a new—equally full and vast—system of thought can do that, and this new system cannot be imported from outside. It must be built from the actual experience of American life, even and especially when that experience seems most random and unintelligible.

Ask any educated audience what the best book on America is and the answer will almost inevitably be Tocqueville's *Democracy in America*. My dissertation advisor at Harvard, Harvey Mansfield, always referred to it as the best book on America and the best book about democracy—the two qualities being necessarily related. After almost two centuries, it remains a powerful theory of the United States. Its influence on more recent examinations of America is obvious and explicit. It is indeed a theory, a broad vision of what distinguishes the American experiment and the forces pushing it from a dramatic founding moment into what already for Tocqueville looked like the coming of a glorious future. It inaugurated the fashion of books about America written by Europeans. Sharing a lot with the new country but benefiting from an external perspective, Tocqueville hoped to unveil one of the biggest mysteries of his and our time. What is America? Why has this country built practically from scratch come to extend its power over the whole planet? What human possibilities does America represent, what did it bring into the world that did not exist before? Leaving on his journey through the United States in 1831, Tocqueville explained that he and his travel companion Gustave de Beaumont were "going with the intention of examining, in detail and as scientifically as possible, all the workings of that vast American society that everyone talks about and no one knows."[4]

After Tocqueville's death, Beaumont described how his friend went about travelling and thinking about what he saw around him in America.

> One can scarcely imagine the activity of body and mind that consumed him like a burning fever and never slackened. Everything was a subject for observation. He would ask in advance, in his head, all the questions he hoped to resolve. Whenever an idea occurred to him, he noted it down without delay, no matter where he was, because he had observed that the force of first impressions can never be recovered if one lets them slip away.[5]

After nine months of relentless exploration—the two friends visited seventeen of the then twenty-four states—Tocqueville set down to explain what it all meant, not only for the United States but for the world. The result was the two volumes of *Democracy in America*, published in 1835 and 1840 respectively.

Tocqueville understands the present moment—and the most present and newest country in the world was America—as the culmination or near culmination of a centuries-old process which becomes clear and intelligible precisely because the possibilities contained at the beginning are now approaching their full development. In other words, he understands the present as a stage in the growth and perfection of modern European history.

He explains on the very first page of *Democracy in America* that he conceived the idea for the book when he realized that the social state existing in America was an extreme version of the social state in Europe, and in Europe things were rapidly advancing towards the same extreme. The process had started in Europe, and Tocqueville is not afraid to locate its beginnings, rather precisely, some 700 years before his time. France was then divided among a few families who possessed the land and governed the inhabitants. At that time, right of command passed from generation to generation by inheritance. Change came first of all within the ranks of the clergy. Open to all, poor and rich alike, it gained political power. Society was becoming less hierarchical. The need for civil laws granted new power to a class of educated jurists. Trade became a source of political power, and finance followed. Greater equality goes together with a new kind of society where knowledge spreads and technology uproots tradition. As Tocqueville puts it, the discovery of firearms equalizes the villein and the noble on the battlefield; printing offers equal resources to their intelligence; the mail comes to deposit enlightenment on the doorstep of the poor man's hut as at the portal of the palace. Tocqueville clearly believes that the political principle of equality inspires these inventions, which are in some sense derivative, but he does not pursue the intriguing possibility that democracy in modern times can be distinguished from its ancient manifestations by the application of the democratic principle to knowledge and science.

This long process of 700 years Tocqueville describes as purely destructive. Democracy has come about as one after another of the great sources of authority crumbled, without being replaced by anything else. We no longer take kings seriously, we deem every aristocratic claim fictive, but nothing has been put in their place. Tocqueville turns to America as the place where the task of destruction has been completed—there was never much to destroy in those lands untouched by civilization—and where the growth of a new democratic form of life can now begin. We have destroyed an aristocratic society and stand amid the debris of the former edifice. It is the worst of times, but also the best of times, where something new can be envisaged.

On their departure from England, the emigrants to America had a very weak conception of inequality. It was hardly the wealthy that would be going into exile, and the land in America was neither likely to build great fortunes nor to dispense with the personal labour and initiative of the landowner. At the same time, these emigrants brought with them a set of ideas which were at the time starting to take hold in the mother country: notions of rights, of local government, and even of the sovereignty of the people were already strong during the Tudor monarchy. The Puritans of New England even carried with them the most absolute democratic and republican theories. All the English colonies were therefore prepared to offer an ideal ground for the development of that "bourgeois and democratic freedom of which the history of the world had still not offered a complete model."[6] Freedom of speech and of the press, individual rights, Parliament's prerogatives—these ideas were transported to America when, in Europe, they were still rare plants. They could grow faster across the Atlantic where they found no opposition.

As James Truslow Adams put in his *The Epic of America*, published in 1931 and written very much in the spirit of Tocqueville, America started as a democracy.

> That was something radically new, though the political philosophy was not. American thinkers had nourished their minds on the great Englishmen, Sydney, Locke, Hobbes, and others. There was nothing novel in their theory. What was novel was the putting of the theory into practice, and that they owed to the American wilderness. They did not need to chop off the head of their king. In the process of the steady chopping down of the interminable forest the need of a king had gone.[7]

So here is what Tocqueville is telling us. By a historical strike of luck, the democratic ideas which were only then starting on their path in England had been transplanted to the New World, where they could grow unimpeded. The historical changes that would in time occur in Europe had happened there much faster, so that when *Democracy in America* was written, it was actually possible to look across the ocean to see the future. Not the future of America, but the future of Europe.

In America democracy is given over to its own inclinations. Its style is natural and all its movements are free. It is there that one must judge it. In other words, Tocqueville finds in America a perfectly pure version of democracy. Since Europeans are themselves moving in that direction, where will they end if not in something like America, once all the remnants of aristocracy and absolute monarchy have been removed?

The problem with Tocqueville—his failure—is the way he takes the rules of political development in Europe as universal. Remember, his was a world ruled by Europe. The great world cities to which artists and financiers flowed were London and Paris, soon to be joined by Berlin. The First Opium War in China was taking place around the time Tocqueville published the second volume of his major work. It was to mark one of the great turning points in world history, and American traders were very much present in Canton—they observed events from a distance, ready to benefit from the outcome but unable to shape it. The years when the United States would be a world leader in technology—with the revolutionary inventions of Thomas Edison and Graham Bell—were still far in the future, the moment when its economy would surpass that of Britain even more distant, and on matters of culture and style America followed Europe. The greatest American writer of the years before Tocqueville's visit, Washington Irving, lived in a state of alienation from his society. Irving despaired that America would be able to produce an accomplished culture, let alone an original one. His sense of alienation led him to spend seventeen of his most productive years in Europe—in England, France and Spain—and to use European literary models in his works. There was nothing else available to him. As for Fenimore Cooper, what were his novels but American versions of the historical romances of Walter Scott?

The English accent was assiduously cultivated in Ivy League universities and Shakespeare was widely read and taught. British tastes remained a mark of distinction, and by the time the struggle for independence became a distant memory, even the monarchy acquired fervent fans and followers. The Boston business elite invested in country estates to emulate English landowners and Southern planters maintained grand Georgian estates.[8] When Henry Adams arrived in London in 1858, fresh from his Harvard education, he noted that "the boys in the streets made such free comments on the American clothes and figures, that the travelers hurried to put on tall hats and long overcoats to escape criticism."

During Tocqueville's lifetime, the American South remained a semi-colonial economic enclave of Britain. Between 1820 and 1860 the United States accounted for 80 per cent of the global production of cotton. Most was exported, and more than half of total exports went to Britain. From this perspective, the Civil War was a second War of Independence, but the South was not alone as a dependent economy.

Tocqueville wrote to his father that in the newspapers "the price of cotton takes up more space than general questions about government." How naive. Cotton was the chief Southern export, a critical link in American economic dependence, the focus of bitter tariff wars and one of the main triggers for the Civil War. He also argues that American ships enjoyed a dominant position in the carrying trade. That changed dramatically with the development of the steamship. Again, he fails to see the larger forces, in this case technological supremacy. Representatives of American shipping interests would be lamenting by 1864 that they were completely dependent on foreign flags for international trade. Most of these foreign flags were British.[9] Finally, and perhaps more importantly, British lines of credit remained so dominant throughout the nineteenth century that nothing of importance could be done without them. As a consequence, the City of London enjoyed enormous influence and leverage over political decisions in Washington. As many suspected, some of this influence was due to bribes paid to American politicians by British interests: Daniel Webster, secretary of state under three presidents, accepted a payment of nine hundred pounds from Baring to help push Maryland to pay its debts to British creditors.[10] Many of the more radical ideas that Andrew Jackson took to the presidency had to be abandoned under pressure from financial and commercial interests. The Austrian economist Friedrich List, writing in 1844, had the United States in mind when he complained that the City "by loans and the receipt of interest in them makes all peoples of the earth her tributaries." When the Bank of England adjusted interest rates, the repercussions were quickly felt across the Atlantic.

The position of the United States was not so different from that of developing countries subject to the impact of American power a century later. Its economy, however, benefited from being included in the vaster sphere of the British Empire. The appropriate analogy here would probably be the spectacular growth trajectory of the Chinese economy over the past few decades. Free of the burdens of an incumbent superpower, it was able to benefit from free trade under favourable conditions, while preparing to assume a greater global political role later in its development. The United States is an earlier example of the process. At the time Tocqueville was writing, it was no more than a peripheral country in the global economic system. Might it be expected to always embody the same values as the empire it was struggling to supersede? Or was the similarity of views then in place a reflex of its peripheral status?

And then the world changed. Overnight, it seemed to some, but in effect over a decade or two. Henry Adams chronicles the process better than anyone else. When he attended the World's Fair in Chicago in 1893, an extravaganza of American industrial and scientific optimism, he commented that for the first time the question was asked whether the American people knew where they were going. Adams tried to answer it—in characteristically cryptic language: "They might still be driving or drifting unconsciously to some point in thought, as their solar system was said to be drifting towards some point in space; and that, possibly, if relations enough could be observed, this point might be fixed." In 1893, perhaps a year or two earlier, the American economy finally exceeded its British rival in size. Adams marvels at the occasion: "One held one's breath at the nearness of what one had never expected to see, the crossing of courses, and the lead of American energies."[11] Colonel Harland Sanders, the brain behind Kentucky Fried Chicken, was born in 1890. Coca-Cola was patented in 1893, that wondrous year of beginnings.

In 1890 the Census Bureau announced the end of the frontier, meaning there was no longer a discernible frontier line in the west, nor any large tracts of land yet unbroken by settlement. In a famous essay published in 1893, Frederick Jackson Turner saw in the advance of American settlement westward a process of Americanization. The wilderness finds a European and leaves him a savage. With each stage in the westward movement civilization has to be built anew, but since a percentage of the original European character is bound to be lost each time, the successive iteration will deliver a new product that is American. The first frontier was the Atlantic seaboard, and it was the frontier of Europe. The colonists were European; Europe ended where the original settlement ended. Moving westward, the frontier became more and more American, a transmutation Tocqueville failed to contemplate. "Thus the advance of the frontier has meant a steady movement away from the influence of Europe, a steady growth of independence on American lines."[12]

By the end of the decade, Henry Adams is again taken by surprise, this time by the newly found American ability to lead on the international stage. The first instance he mentions is the Boxer Rebellion in China. The United States finds itself in a desperate situation, with Secretary of State John Hay looking on as Russia and Germany seem poised to control the whole of China. And then it was Adams that looked on: "When Hay suddenly ignored European leadership, took the lead himself, rescued the Legations and saved China, Adams looked on, as incredulous as Europe, though not quite so stupid, since, on that branch of education, he knew enough for his purpose."[13] By January 1904, on the eve of the Russo-Japanese war, he is astonished to find out, on entering Washington, that his country now thinks as a world power.

Cultural influence came more slowly, as it always does, and when it arrived—as a late bloom of technological and industrial prowess—it again came as a shock to the very Americans who had dreamed about that day for almost a century. An anecdote from Harold Loeb: when the American met Marinetti in Milan, Loeb told him how much Americans looked up to Europe, to England, Russia and France for literature, to Germany for music, and to France and Italy for the plastic arts. In return, the founder of Futurism burst into rhetoric extolling America. To his mind, nearly everything important in his day came out of the United States. "He cited our skyscrapers, movies, jazz, even machinery and the comics." And in Rome, Loeb listened to the French writer Blaise Cendrars praising all things American, "machines and jazz, comics and the cinema."[14]

Tocqueville is not wrong when he uses America as a mirror in which Europe can spy its own future—but the claim should be interpreted in an entirely different way from what he has in mind. Tocqueville is blind to the question of civilization. He believes in a single history organized around a common end point. His political world is the world of the epic rather than the novel. He fails to see how history is made of multiple stories, different visions of the whole developing in patterns not so different from those of an individual life.

His failure is a failure of imagination. He can conceive of America as the end point of European culture and politics, the denouement of a historical commandment, but he cannot see that America is meant to outgrow Europe and create its own distinctive path. He praises the energy and vitality of American life and yet fails to understand that this energy and vitality cannot be satisfied by imitating an older civilization. His book is a book about Europe, not a book about America, the very last of the European visions of the New World, written just before the prophetic words of Emerson, Thoreau, Melville and Whitman announcing that America was a beginning rather than an end. In *Democratic Vistas*, published in 1871, Whitman asked: "We see the sons and daughters of the New World, ignorant of its genius, not yet inaugurating the native, the universal and the near, still importing the distant, the partial and the dead. We see London, Paris, Italy—not original, superb, as where they belong—but second-hand here, where they do not belong. We see the shreds of Hebrews, Romans, Greeks; but where, on her own soil, do we see, in any faithful, highest, proud expression, America herself?"

In later years Tocqueville would become rather critical of what he saw as the "spirit of adventure" in America, its pride in strength, which pushed the young republic into the acquisition of Texas and California, and the first inchoate dreams of world empire. That history was after all not coming to an end in America, that it might in fact be starting anew, was a great cause of anxiety for Tocqueville. "What is certain", he wrote to an American correspondent in 1856, "is that in Europe the idea that you are approaching rapidly the time of revolution is more and more accepted and is spreading very quickly." The pages of *Democracy in America* remain to this day a pious but lifeless portray of mankind at the end of history, the cyclical return to a simple, rustic, bucolic and virtuous pastoral. America as Arcadia.

Remarkably, Tocqueville goes so far as to claim that the taste for material enjoyments does not bring democratic man to the excesses of aristocracy. In democracies, he says, it is not a question of building vast palaces or depleting nature to pursue our desires, but only of making life slightly more convenient. Even the very rich will be like that, he insists. As a statement about America or about democracy, it was and remains curiously implausible, fantastic, risible.

Tocqueville saw in America more than America itself, but what he saw was Europe and its imagined future. A more restless mind would have seen in America the movement of civilization, the stages of its early years when imitation reigns, but also the unbridled ambition that pushes each new civilization to outgrow, test and transgress its limits.

Already at the time he was writing, the question that should have occupied Tocqueville was the question of Europe and America, the relations between the two, the initial signs that America would eventually surpass Europe, and the reaction to be expected from the declining power. He ignores this question, because he refuses to consider America as anything but a part of the European world. At most, in some short passages at the end of the first volume of *Democracy in America*, he is able to entertain the thought that America may rise to the leading position in this world. Americans may excel in the application of European principles—the way they have become the best followers of Descartes without ever reading him—but not in the invention of new principles.

There are other errors that follow from this fundamental misconception. When Tocqueville comes upon particularly significant distinguishing traits between Europe and America—the fact, for example, that Americans see no contradiction between democracy and religion—he is invariably led to the conclusion that the American practice is truer to the spirit of democracy. It is all part of his fundamental myth: because in America only democrats exist and the growth of democracy faces few or no obstacles, it must be more perfectly realized there. He thinks like a revolutionary. The ideal state of revolution is the empty canvas upon which a new social and political state can be drawn. In America democracy found an empty canvas—while in Europe it had to battle with all the institutions of the old regime—so we should turn to America for an accurate picture of the democratic regime. And yet he knows, he even affirms it, that the American regime is a copy or replica of ideas only fully explored in Europe. Civilizations, understood as bodies of ideas and beliefs, develop slowly from within themselves. When they reach the full extension of their powers, they are copied, imitated, their prestige may attract the whole planet to their orbit—for a time at least—but these copies are of necessity imperfect. They lack the confidence and understanding of the original. America, while it lived in Europe's shadow, remained one such case. The temptations of Europe were irresistible.

Tocqueville often seems puzzled that Americans are able to reconcile democracy and religion. He has seen the logic of opposition dominate every French discussion. Democracy disposes men to want to judge everything by themselves and to doubt every external authority. Can it be reconciled with religious authority? Tocqueville sees in America the living proof that it can, and he busies himself explaining why. Perhaps the logic of opposition results from the heat of the struggle between two authorities. In America the struggle has been resolved and democrats can afford to be magnanimous towards religion. They may also sense that religion is helpful in tempering the worst excesses of passion and individualism, which can turn against democracy itself. These are the explanations Tocqueville considers. He seems unaware that religion may have thrived in the United States because the democratic principle, as he defines it, was less pure and less rigorously applied there. Americans copied Cartesian doubt more or less haphazardly; they never embraced it.

Or take the case of what Tocqueville calls individualism, the tendency in democratic societies disposing each citizen to isolate himself from the mass of those like him and to withdraw to one side with his family and his friends, so as to create a little society of his own. This Tocqueville regards as a great danger—social ties elevate the individual and render state power less threatening—and he fears that European democracies, caught in the vortex of revolution, will be unable to ward it off. Americans, however, have fought individualism with freedom and they have defeated it: political life, so vibrant and active at all levels in

America, forces citizens to act together and to make them feel every day that they depend on one another.

Again we must ask whether Tocqueville is not looking at the historical picture upside down. With the benefit of retrospection, we now understand that individualism is indeed a fundamental trait of modern democratic societies and we understand better than Tocqueville that it can be regarded as a virtue just as easily as a vice, that social ties can limit creativity and individuality. We also know that the link Tocqueville saw between individualism and the loss of political freedom is much weaker and doubtful than he argued. Finally, it seems clear to us that, to a very great extent, Americans have forgotten the art of association enthused by Tocqueville.

Or, finally, take slavery. That this institution of an older world—so contrary to modern civilization and modern industrial development—survived in America and dictated so much of its social order should have been enough to suggest that the United States remained in fundamental respects an archaic society, with echoes of the vast Asian despotic states; that its future form was still hidden. Incredibly, Tocqueville describes America as a society free of contradictions, more advanced than Europe itself. About slavery he has little of consequence to say.

All these facts conspire to convince us that the distinctively American art of association described and theorized in *Democracy in America* was so far from being a late bloom of democracy that it was in fact a pre-existing condition. Europe may have had its prehistory of social and political forms, but so did America. Much of what Tocqueville praised as the future of modern democracy now seems to us elements of natural or traditional society, which in the United States in the middle of the nineteenth century had yet to go through the demonic mill of democratic transformation. As Henry Adams put it, "the American boy of 1854 stood nearer the year 1 than to the year 1900."

Does this mean that Tocqueville could not have written a great book about America, that it was simply too early to attempt such a task? I do not think so.

Even before Tocqueville set foot in America, Hegel was writing in the solitude of his Berlin studio that "North America will be comparable to Europe only after the immeasurable space which that country presents to its inhabitants shall have been occupied, and the members of the political body shall have begun to be pressed back on each other." America was still in the process of creating a modern civil society and an organized state. What has taken place there until that moment, Hegel says, "is only an echo of the Old World." A time will come when something new will arise, but that is impossible to guess. But at just the same time Tocqueville was writing the second of his two volumes, Emerson thought it proper to write about America as America and to try to look into the future of the country as a new beginning. He senses the vital energy around him and knows that it will be used to tread new paths. Perhaps these will at first turn out to be mistaken, forcing one to start anew, but all that is part and parcel of the game of civilization. And, of course, this is a game one must play. Whether America becomes a new beginning is not a question to be observed but one to be decided in action. There is something of the future American mode of thought in the way Emerson affirms that courage and action are virtues not only for the man of action but also for the scholar, the writer, the artist. He may well have been the first pragmatist, even though he was many other things besides.

Emerson does more than this. As his scalpel dissects the foreign civilization that America is now struggling to escape, he finds a way to overcome it. Tocqueville plays a sacrificial role here because Emerson wants his countrymen to embrace individualism with renewed passion. He suspects that modern society points towards individualism as an ideal and that Europeans do not live up to the promise. Attracted by individualism, they simultaneously evade it. Like Tocqueville, they want to temper it. Everything that tends to isolate the individual tends to greatness, Emerson says. It is impossible that Tocqueville did not know about these thoughts when he published the second volume of *Democracy in America*, three years after they were expressed. While Tocqueville wants America to stand for a more moderate version of modern social tastes, Emerson would like to embrace the future more vigorously.

After all, these were the decades when nationalism swept over Europe. In the constricted space of the old continent, every nation felt forced to define itself against its neighbours, and the machinery of collectivization was put in motion. Education, the press, mores, all were directed to create citizens and make them play their part in the national work. Did America escape some of these developments? It is possible. It had no neighbours to fear. Emerson concludes his address "The American Scholar" by lamenting the fate of those who, rather than being their own measure, are reckoned in the hundreds or the thousands, members of a party or a nation, their opinions "predicted geographically". The alternative he seeks: man shall treat with man as sovereign state with sovereign state. Emerson seems to think in terms of a grand contest between Europe and America to decide which of the two will be able to realize the implicit promise of modern society. In "Self-Reliance" he recalls an answer he gave when quite young to an elder who was wont to importune him with the dear old doctrines of the Church. On saying, "What have I to do with the sacredness of traditions, if I live wholly from within?" his older friend suggested, "But these impulses may be from below, not from above." Emerson replied, "They do not seem to me to be such; but if I am the Devil's child, I will live then from the Devil." And then he says: never imitate. Why care for Europe, for Rome, for Egypt? If the American artist will love the "precise thing" to be done here and now in America, then "taste and sentiment will be satisfied".

Tocqueville is never able to free himself from the perspective of European civilization; he studies it as the final political form in human history, and looks for its full development in America, which is given the role of resolving democracy's contradictions. It does not occur to him that both Europe and America are individual stories developing within a much larger history of different political civilizations, an empty space with no predefined paths: the game of civilization. At the bottom of the gulf in perception separating them is the way Emerson sees America as a beginning, Tocqueville as an end.

For me, many of the issues discussed here were crystallized in a conversation in Delhi with my friend Krishnan Srinivasan, former Indian foreign secretary. I had spoken of a division between the European and Asian worlds—the main topic of a previous book—and Krishnan corrected me by saying that it would be more appropriate to speak of the American and Asian worlds. My argument: there is no American world as such because everything about the United States goes back to European civilization with its fundamental outlook of democratic, liberal, capitalist and scientific values. America may be more powerful, but in that case nothing more follows than the realization that the European world is ruled from Washington. I was repeating Tocqueville. Back then that was still my starting point. As European civilization expanded more or less to the whole planet, it may have found its strongest expression outside the geographic boundaries of Europe. Tocqueville sometimes calls Americans the "English race in America".

This is one way of looking at the question, no doubt, but as I reflected on that conversation afterwards, it started to look like a very poor way to consider it. If political and economic power are now located across the Atlantic, why not accept the fact with all the consequences that follow from it, including the implausibility of America's continuing cultural and intellectual dependence on European ideas? It was easier for an Indian like Srinivasan than for me to see through the pious fiction that American hegemony in Europe is not really hegemony because the two regions are too alike. He saw the American legions in Europe and the disproportionate international clout of the dollar. Those facts spoke for themselves.

Emerson thought that America could become more European than Europe and more successful at being European. But do things work like this in the game of civilization? Can you be successful without being successful in your own way? As Whitman put it in *Democratic Vistas*, a great moral civilization is the only justification of a great material one. Like its political government, the civilization of America must extricate itself from even the greatest models of the past and, while courteous to them, must have entire faith in itself and in the products of its own original spirit only. Nothing less than the mightiest original sovereign civilization has ever really led the world. But even Whitman and Emerson remain essentially European in their outlook. We must turn to a later writer to find someone with a genuine claim to knowledge of America and to be regarded as its prophet.

"All very beautiful and promising," William James wrote in his diary when he arrived in Palo Alto. He had been invited to head the philosophy department of the recently created Stanford University. As the pre-eminent name in American philosophy at the time, James was under no pressing need to move to California, where the frontier spirit was still alive, a place more attractive to those in search of fortune than knowledge. He must have been attracted by the adventure and novelty of the empty land. No history, no past. "You can hear the historic silence," he wrote to his wife. As for the students, James hoped that he would find minds without preconceptions. He soon learned that he was right, but perhaps in an extreme way, as even the basic words of philosophical language were unknown in California.

The year was 1906, a date which must bring to mind the great and terrible San Francisco earthquake. On the early morning of 18 April much of Stanford would be demolished. James, who was already awake, noticed that the bed began to waggle. For close to a minute the quake shook his room "exactly as a terrier shakes a rat." Then an awful roaring noise filled the air, before everything went silent again. Only the babble of human voices remained behind. In an essay written weeks later, James recalls that his feelings during that terrible minute were mostly of glee, delight, welcome. Delight at the renewed sense that the world is so much more vivid than words and concepts, at the gulf separating the idea of an earthquake from its concrete reality. "Go it," James felt like crying, "and go it stronger." For James it felt like the earthquake came directly to him. "To me, it wanted simply to manifest the meaning of its name."[15] A better philosophy lesson, he seems to be saying, than those he had come to California to deliver.

The earthquake revealed to James a world that was pure direction, pure flux, having nothing fixed or stable in it. In place of the mythological world of concepts, James builds a world of hammering energies and active experience. The meaning of things, like the meaning of the earthquake, is contained in their experience, so James finds himself asking for stronger and deeper experiences in his search for knowledge. Towards the end of *Pragmatism*, published a year after the quake, he writes that he finds himself willing to take the universe to be really dangerous and adventurous with real losses and real losers. Even then one must play.[16] While Henry Adams wrote lyrically about his failure to understand a world made new by technology and progress, James explained that without embracing the forces of change, no genuine understanding is possible.

TWO

When he wants to give a final character to reality, he finds it not in objects or in consciousness but in the way all the parts of experience hang together from one to the next. Experience has its own concatenated or continuous structure. Whether something is true or false depends on whether it can be lived or experienced. Stories make up the ultimate ground of reality. James argues, for example, that if one takes a single moment, nothing can be distinguished from everything else. Once we release the flow of time, however, different realities go on their separate paths. I stop writing on the desk and move on to other dealings, while the desk may be carried off by someone else. My identity and the identity of the desk consist of these separate stories and nothing else.

Up to about 1850, James says, everyone believed that science expressed truths that were exact copies of reality. But suddenly there were so many geometries, so many logics, so many physical and chemical hypotheses, so many classifications, each one of them good for so much and yet not good for everything, that the notion that even the truest formula may be a human device and not a literal copy has dawned upon us. Which are true? Those that work, those that can go out into the world and fare well in dealing with reality in all its aspects. Other truths will be created and they too will struggle to survive. Owing to the fact that all experience is a process, no point of view can ever be the last one. Reality genuinely grows. Truth is life on the frontier.

The only real guarantee we have against false thinking is the pressure of experience itself, which makes us sick of errors and collapses our illusions. When it was possible to live in obedience to the belief that the moon and sun were deities, then these beliefs were true. Today we cannot live like that, so those beliefs are false. Some ideas are helpful for life, they guide us in its practical struggles. As James put it, if there is a life that is better for us and if any idea will help us lead that life, then that idea is true. This is a remarkably open theory. So much can be equally true for James: his philosophy has no prejudices, no dogmas, no canons. How democratic and how American. It is even able to reconcile philosophy and religion. After all, if the idea of God fits our life, if it guides us in leading a full life—if it fits every part of life, if it makes life more living and richer—then the idea of God is true, because what other kind of truth could there be? As we shall see, this is exactly how religion in America must be understood. How well James captures its spirit, even in its current manifestations, and how defective Tocqueville is by comparison.[17]

Truth here means something rather similar to the coherence and strength of a plot line. It organizes experience. James notes, for instance, how the idea of a substance separate from its attributes is almost always metaphysical nonsense, except in the case of the Catholic mass, where we need the idea of substance to organize the story of how the wafer preserves all its qualities while being transformed into the body of Christ. The only way to make this work is to say that the change was in the substance, not the attributes, so the idea of substance is a good and true one here. The real question for us is: What is the world going to be? What is life eventually to make of itself? What must we accept in order to bring about new experiences, new lives? That the past existed is guaranteed by its coherence with the present, and the present in turn will be tested and modified by the future. Truth is lived, experienced and then discovered in the later revelations of the story. We plunge forward into the field of fresh experience with old beliefs; these determine what we notice; what we notice determines what we do; what we do again determines what we experience, and we build the flux out. The question for James is how interesting, how valuable, how worthy is the story, the new addition to reality.[18] Reality is essentially a theatre for heroism. Call it the Hollywood theory of truth.

46

TWO

James is of course familiar with the history of European philosophy, and he tentatively places his work within that tradition. Where else could he place it? But he is acutely aware that his project is a new beginning, or else a failure. He is not sure that he has been successful in starting a whole new chapter in the history of philosophy, but he entertains that thought and never abandons hope. He is at his most revolutionary when stubbornly resisting the notion of a final truth in ethics and politics. The history of European philosophy—and it does not matter in this case if we place the beginning in classical Athens or modern Florence—is a repeated attempt to find that final truth, to build a final system of thought. James hears that siren call, but he resists it. There is no truth, but many truths. His liberalism is a liberalism of thought. It does not create a general philosophy allowing people to go on with their separate lives. It wants to build a world where—the difference between life and philosophy being illusory—people can go on with their separate lives and their separate philosophies.

James does not argue that there is no truth; he argues that there are many truths and that they are equally good and wholesome, even when they contradict each other. Truth for him is a way of life and there are many different ways to live. Think of this world as a large, palatial hotel with many and perhaps infinite rooms. In one a person may live according to the dictates of religion. In a second a scientist spends his years looking for the secrets of the universe. In a third an artist composes a poem or a symphony or transforms his allotted room into an installation. In a fourth a system of metaphysics is being excogitated, and in a fifth the impossibility of metaphysics is being shown.[19] In order to enter or leave their respective rooms, the guests must pass through the floor corridor. But what is the corridor? Only the space necessary to keep the rooms separate, nothing more.

THREE

The American Invaders. A book with that title, published by a mainstream British author in 1902, described how it all started. "America has invaded Europe not with armed men, but with manufactured products." Shaving soap, electric motors, the shoe industry, the match industry, machine tools: American industrialists were clearing the field. Even British jokes were machine-made in the offices of New York publishers.

Only ten years before—the author marvelled—Britain took raw products from America, exporting its own manufactured goods across the Atlantic. Now the situation had been turned around. And industry was only the beginning. Already New York was superseding London as the financial capital of the world. "The expansion of American trade has prepared the field for American bankers, and now, late in the day, American capital is being launched in bulk in the establishment of trading banks abroad."[1] The previous generation of Americans had rushed west in search of fortune. The current one was going east. Britain was the natural landing patch, but similar accounts of the sudden arrival and rush of people and goods were being recorded in Austria, Germany, Belgium, even Russia. To someone reading them today, they are reminiscent of the accounts given by American writers of "the Japanese invaders" of the Reagan years or "the Chinese invaders" in our own time.

From this moment dates the lasting fear of what Europeans were quick to call Americanization. For many this was more or less equivalent to the end of times or, at least, the end of everything sacred. What America was exporting to Europe was not just its manufacturing prowess. It was a whole way of life, fundamentally antithetical to European civilization because the only goals it recognized were profit and efficiency. Taste would be sacrificed because everything must be produced for the greatest number according to the maxims of the assembly line. Leisure would disappear and be replaced by the divine cult of work and productivity. Tradition must be uprooted because tradition is full of wasteful or inefficient practices. There was the accusation of Puritanism as well, but even here no European would dream of blaming America of excessive spirituality: Puritan prohibitions concerning alcohol or sex were seen as pre-emptive measures to create the most efficient workers, and reduce human beings to machines. As Antonio Gramsci put it, the history of industrialism was a painful and bloody process of subjugating natural instincts to more rigid norms of order, precision and discipline. In America the rationalization of work and prohibition were undoubtedly connected. Prohibition was part of "the biggest collective effort to date to create, with unprecedented speed, and with a consciousness of purpose unmatched in history, a new type of worker and of man." And as for sex: "It seems clear that the new industrialism wants monogamy: it wants the man as worker not to squander his nervous energies in the disorderly and stimulating pursuit of occasional sexual satisfaction."[2]

Much of the rising anti-Americanism had a class origin. The American model of production was an engine of standardization. Rich and poor might differ in what they could buy, but the products were available to all and the very logic of profit dictated that as many people as possible should have access to them. A society where everyone works is a society where no fundamental distinction between classes can survive. Many European conservatives in the decades before the Second World War found the idea distasteful. Others found it terrifying. By blaming America for transformations that were strictly connected to the development of modern society, they were able to entertain the illusion that these transformations could be stopped or even reversed. "When the mask fell, the Europeans saw their latest selves: they preferred to think they were seeing the face of the United States."[3] To the extent that America represented the end point of modern European civilization, it raised new anxieties in Europe. All the vital creativity and openness of historical development seemed to have disappeared. A century ago Europeans were already learning to resent America because it stood for the most dreadful of nightmares: the end of history and the American salesman.

For a while, however, there seemed to be a balance. America might be the dominant manufacturing power in the world, but it lagged in military power—the American army was the nineteenth largest in the world in 1913—and its cultural achievements were generally derided in Europe. That changed with the First World War. Keyserling saw it as the birth moment of real America: "Before the War, America still essentially considered herself a colony of Europe, or at least one of many parts of a unified Western World."[4] Mowrer writes with consummate realism that victory in war changes the way we look at a country. Even its literature and arts appear in a different light. "Military triumph always carried its prestige over into other areas."[5] It happened with the Spanish conquistadores, with France under the Bourbons, with Germany after 1870. And it was the case with the United States after 1918. In sheer numbers the American military presence on the Western Front—in the East the "doughboys" were never deployed—was modest, but by conducting a major war an ocean away and coming out of it relatively unscathed, America left no doubts who the main victor in the contest really was.

The journalist Walter Lippmann argued just one day after America entered the war that President Wilson had created an opportunity without parallel: "Through force of circumstances and through his own genius he has made it a practical possibility that he is to be the first great statesman to begin the better organization of the world."[6] This did not happen, in large measure because America still saw itself as part of the old European order—perhaps the most important piece of that puzzle, but not sufficiently powerful or sufficiently interested in replacing a system from which it had benefited more than anyone else. Woodrow Wilson did announce a programme of liberal internationalism in his famous address to Congress in January 1918, but the political will to overcome European resistance was lacking. Bolshevik Russia had plans of its own for world politics, and the British and French regarded the Fourteen Points as a form of utopianism. The first sitting American president to visit Europe, Wilson arrived at Versailles full of optimism. He left after being defeated on every major point of substance. The old order survived. The rhetoric at the Peace Conference was Wilsonian, "but the practice remained that of British imperialism."[7]

In 1918 the United States had a golden opportunity, unprecedented in all history, to assume the leadership of the world, but that opportunity was allowed to pass. There was no sense at that moment that Europe was a spent force in world history. As the American soldiers returned home, they brought with them the vivid impression of European civilization in all its glory: rich cultures whose mysteries were so hard to penetrate and which offered delicate pleasures to the connoisseur, noble cities and landscapes developed over centuries, an explosion of lifestyles and individual freedoms in daily life that few Americans could dream about. Many of these soldiers never returned to America. Europe had walked to the abyss, but the heights from which it had leaped, those were heights America had yet to reach. It was a delicate question where the world was going. Would Europe learn from the war and rebuild its civilization? Would America take its place? As a French author asked in the title of a popular book, "Who will be master, Europe or America?"[8] America or Europe?

Would America—from the heights of its newly acquired powers—reconcile itself to a world order managed by Europeans? In a way this was the most important question to come out of Versailles. Many speculated that a new war might be necessary to conclude the transition to an American empire, and Bertrand Russell even contemplated the possibility that it might take place between the United States and Great Britain. Alternatively, if the British kept their minds, they should voluntary cede the management of the world to their American cousins.[9] In the meantime, the American navy began developing plans to handle a war against both Britain and Japan. Churchill believed Britain was about to "drift into direct naval rivalry with the United States."[10]

As it turned out, the question was evaded or ignored. The existing European order was kept in place—to do or die, as luck dictated. If it was a defeat for Europeans to appease Hitler, it was an even greater defeat to allow things to get to a point where "the German people found itself in such a frame of mind that it could, without great resistance or remonstrance, accept a Hitler as its leader and master."[11] It *was* a European defeat: every concatenation of events leading to the fateful outcome was the product of choices made in Germany, in France and in Britain during the interwar years. The United States had very little to do with it.

Europe had shown itself wholly incapable of managing the world's affairs, yet was left in a position to do just that. Britain and France emerged from the First World War with their empires intact and even enlarged. Global events continued to be dictated by the iron logic of European power rivalry. Countries with colonial empires were able to deny their rivals access to markets and commodities. As the status quo was increasingly challenged by Japan, Italy and Germany, the world turned a blind eye to their incursions into China, Abyssinia and Central Europe. Many in Britain believed that the best way to preserve peace was to abandon the balance of power policy and offer revisionist powers their own spheres of influence in an attempt to mollify them. It was a supremely dangerous game and the consequences were catastrophic.

In a famous article in *Life* in 1941, Henry Luce passionately argued for a course correction. There was a new European war and the United States could not avoid being in it. Not out of a desire for survival, but because the war gave it the opportunity— a second opportunity and thus one not to be missed—to assume leadership in the world. The fundamental trouble with America was, as Luce saw it, that whereas their country had become in the course of the twentieth century the most powerful and the most vital nation in the world, nevertheless Americans were unable to accommodate themselves spiritually and practically to that fact. Their failure to exert upon the world the full impact of their influence was invariably connected to the tragedies of the age. Luce seems to blame America for those tragedies, but only through its aversion to power and its exercise. "Roosevelt must succeed where Wilson failed."[12]

Someone had to rule the world and very clearly the nations of Europe were no longer plausible candidates for the task. Without exception they would come out of the Second World War abased and humiliated, their proud histories shattered by the voluntary embrace of monstrous regimes or the impotence to defeat them on the battlefield. Even Britain, never having surrendered to Hitler, could not ignore that on its own it would inevitably have been defeated—as Churchill so clearly put it, victory would not be possible until "the New World, with all its power and might, steps forth to the rescue and the liberation of the old"—or that Nazi Germany so often presented the British settlement of India as the model for its planned colonization of the conquered Ukrainian and Russian lands.

In early 1945 *The New York Times* ran a piece calling Europe the "New Dark Continent". This time the returning American soldiers would not stop to contemplate the noble ruins of a great civilization. The whole continent was a pile of rubble. Masses of displaced persons roamed barren country fields, many collapsing of starvation on the sides of the road. There were the piles of gassed dead bodies at Auschwitz and Buchenwald. Tens of thousands of abandoned orphans congregated in city squares, waiting for help that would never arrive. In cities like Berlin, Rome, Vienna and even London, American soldiers spent their days going through waiting lines of women on the streets, women for whom prostitution was now the only possible way to survive. The literary critic Edmund Wilson wrote a book detailing his impressions of Europe in 1945. There is a lot about prostitution—including his own meetings with young women—but not much else.[13] Or rather, above everything else, guilt and shame: shame for having destroyed the best of an incomparable world civilization; guilt for having produced an incomparable record of atrocities. When Secretary of State George Marshall asked his newly created Policy Planning Staff to prepare a report on the situation in Europe, George Kennan delivered a text describing the impact of the war on the economic, political and social structure of Europe, yet the impact went much deeper, having exhausted the continent's "spiritual vigor". The phrase did not make it into the speech at Harvard where Marshall announced the plan for Europe's economic recovery which would soon carry his name.[14]

In the conclusion to his book Edmund Wilson expressed the hitherto unfamiliar opinion—among intellectuals—that the

United States was now politically more advanced than any other part of the world, Europe included. He did not mean it in a material sense. It was in "democratic creativeness", the ability to develop a new politics adapted to change and movement, that Americans had shown themselves superior to others. Europe could no longer be regarded as a sanctuary of high culture to which American literary talent escaped and much less a standard inspiring and justifying a criticism of American life. Had Hitler or Stalin provided an open field for human creativity and the free play of intellect? In the spring of 1938, Thomas Mann travelled across America delivering a lecture titled "The Coming Victory of Democracy", published in book form that same year. In the concluding pages to the lecture the great German novelist made a claim with which he intended to give a jolt to his American audience:

> I was delighted with the atmosphere that I found here, because it was almost free of the poisons that fill the air of Europe—because here, in contrast to the cultural fatigue and inclination to barbarism prevalent in the Old World, there exists a joyful respect for culture, a youthful sensitivity to its values and its products.[15]

The American philistine had become the European philistine. The wheel had come full circle. Or to put it differently: even if one disagreed that American culture had become better, the world had certainly become worse. As Arthur Schlesinger put it, "next to Himmler, even Babbitt began to look good." I will return to Babbitt below.

The poet Allan Dowling had written a text in 1932—he was living in France at the time—lambasting American culture and comparing it to the riches of France, where political leaders befriended great artists: "My countrymen have too little respect for the soul. They have never honored a poet or a painter as they honor Ford and Rockefeller and Lindbergh, or a nonentity like Coolidge." The result? "That France, with its genial culture and appreciation of the fine arts, is in the forefront of the world today" while "those poor United States, so full of promise, are headed for more terrible days than they have known already. They will not listen. They despise everything that is noble and beautiful." Harsh words. He wrote them in 1932. By 1952, two decades later, Dowling had taken them back. The whole atmosphere of the country had changed or so it seemed to him: hero-worshipping of the businessman had ended with the Depression and the government seemed increasingly on the side of painters, writers and musicians. The vast movement of people transported to Europe during and after the First World War had, upon their return, brought new ideas and a new spirit of cosmopolitanism to the narrow confines of American life. A growing number of Americans studied abroad, and tourism exploded. All this was recognized and accepted. More important, perhaps, "in the meantime, in Europe, dictatorships increased and freedom faded." As the literary critic Leslie Fiedler saw it, the new American abroad now found a Europe racked by self-pity, as alienated from its traditions as Milwaukee or Des Moines and haunted by the idea of America. "A hundred years after the Manifesto the specter that is haunting Europe is—Gary Cooper!" Philip Rahv, co-founder of *Partisan Review*—where these reflections on Europe and America were published—returned to Henry James and his vision of Europe as the "rich, deep and dark Old World" to note that only the darkness was left. Perhaps European culture still had a future, but what it was able to produce at present—the languishing efforts of pre-existing currents such as existentialism—was of a scale and importance "insufficient to compel our attention or to provoke meaningful reactions in American culture." Jacques Barzun, the great historian of ideas, put it best when he wrote: "In short, by 1945, America having won a war on both her oceans, and finding itself involved in the four quarters of the world, was quite simply *the* world power, which means: the center of world awareness: it was Europe that was provincial."[16]

For the New World, it was a fundamentally new situation. Europe no longer stood as the perennial model against which its own ways should be measured. A new transatlantic community could be built without the obstacles of the interwar years. Both sides agreed who should lead it, and there was a common enemy—the Soviet Union—against whom their efforts could be directed. But over time, differences were bound to appear. For there was, after all, a contradiction at the heart of the new transatlantic world. The centre of military and political power lay in America, but the core principles inspiring its action were still the principles of European civilization. Think of it this way. Industrial prowess had been the first to migrate across the Atlantic; then economic power; next, military might; and, at the very end, political leadership. What remained in Europe were the values, the political principles, the philosophical vision.

Could that vision last? Could Europe remain in relation to America what Greece had been to Rome? And could the new Rome renounce the old call—manifest destiny in all its truth—to bring a new type of civilization into being? These were real, perhaps even open questions—to the happy few who understood the game of civilization. Slowly the new centre of world power was beginning to pursue its own instincts in complete freedom. The ruling ideas had been deposed and new ones had to take their place. It should not surprise us that just as America developed the power to shape events in Europe, it should also develop a markedly different outlook on the world from the European one.

In or about 1945 the United States became a European power. The expansion of the European sphere to accommodate a powerful outside actor had happened before. At some point, we remember, Russia too had become a European power. Perhaps that was already the case with Peter the Great, perhaps it came to pass later in the eighteenth century with Catherine. The European system of power changed after that, but Russia had become a European power by becoming European, so the whole process came to signify an expansion of Europe's borders. No such destiny awaited the United States.

When the question of political power was finally posed, it had acquired an urgent character: either the United States took over the reins in Europe or the Soviet Union would. The latter scenario seemed catastrophic. A new world war would become inevitable and America would have to fight it alone. Under the pressure of events, a number of decisions were quickly taken that would link America and Europe closer together than at any other time in the past. The Marshall Plan set in motion a process of economic recovery in Western Europe—including West Germany—and Nato was created with the explicit aim of placing the United States in charge of European security. After the war in Korea provided fresh evidence that the Soviet Union could act aggressively in pursuit of its aims, Washington moved four additional divisions to Germany. In September 1950 the North Atlantic Council agreed on the establishment of an integrated force under centralized command, "adequate to deter aggression and to ensure the defense of Western Europe." The force would have a Supreme Allied Commander. As Eisenhower was appointed to the new post, the first units of the new deployments arrived in Germany. By the end of 1951 most of the deployment had been completed. By 1954 there were over 350,000 American troops in Europe.

Some have compared the Marshall Plan to a structural adjustment programme. Even the grants were not exactly free money. In return for vital help in furthering its economic recovery, the United States expected Europe to mend its ways, abandoning the old habits of economic nationalism and central planning and replacing them with something much closer to the American system: free enterprise, a vast continental market—a market big enough to justify modern methods of cheap production for mass consumption—and the canonization of economic growth as the supreme social goal. The dollar had already become the main global currency. European countries needed access to finance in order to buy essential imports and support their currencies. Later they would find that their banking systems were as dependent on the dollar as their basic consumption needs had been in those postwar years.

All these developments have lost their lustre through the passage of time and excessive familiarity, but to contemporaries they seemed momentous. Europe had collapsed under its own weight. The former centre of world power was now under the absolute control of what had originally been no more than a remote dependency of European civilization. In much of the developing world, those were the years of decolonization, a process filled with its own perversions and distempers. In Europe and America, decolonization had a more vivid and much less ambiguous meaning. The United States was free from European influence. It had reached the promised land by acquiring a new kind of imperium over its former master.

As Roosevelt honed his vision for the postwar world order, his priority was to "bring about a radical reduction in the weight of Europe, in effect to preside over its indefinite retirement from the international scene." Already in January 1941—almost a full year before America even entered the war—he had communicated to the British that the United States regarded the postwar settlement as its particular preserve. De Gaulle's recollections of his talks at the White House in July 1944 indicate that he fully understood the consequences of that vision, "an imposing one although disquieting for Europe and for France."[17] The initial disquiet would never really leave him. As for Churchill, Walter Russell Mead is essentially correct when he writes that the great statesman was able to defend the British Empire against Hitler and Hirohito but was no match for Roosevelt.[18]

American power in Europe was now so present and inescapable—so inescapable in fact that it seemed more like a natural than a political force—that some like the French political scientist Maurice Duverger felt inclined to argue that "there is only one immediate danger for Europe, and that is American civilization."[19] In one area alone the United States continued to trail Europe, as it did in the interwar period. Unlike mass production and mass culture—what Duverger meant by American civilization—social and political thought continued to flow primarily from east to west. European intellectuals of all stripes dreamed of transforming and even transcending capitalism. Europe was the undisputed leader in the theory and practice of revolution, and those Americans who felt its appeal went on learning tours, witnessing in person how the British Labour Party build a modern welfare state in record time, how Paris intellectuals perfected Marxist ideas or, in rare cases, how the Soviet Union planned to create a paradise on Earth. American politics and political thought attracted very little interest in Europe, the same Europe that quickly fell in love with Hollywood movies. And in the meantime, without any theory or even much thought, the United States was able to come out of the Depression and address its political failures. These were very different worlds indeed.

Social and revolutionary ideas had a long historical pedigree in Europe and in a way they fed on themselves: revolutionary agitation created the very phenomena of social conflict and economic stasis which could then be presented as evidence that social relations were not working in their current form. The history of European modernity is a relentless search for the society of the future, a society resolving present contradictions. To all appearances, that process is far from concluded. It has changed, no doubt. After the destruction and moral horrors of the Second

World War, Europeans have been looking for political truth in directions diametrically opposite to those tried before. But the search continues and seems as restless as ever. The end of borders, the abdication of the nation state, the pure technocracy of the European Union: from a historical point of view they are radical ideas.

Americans arrived late at the game and, when they did, it seemed less like a game and more like the road to chaos and destruction. With the benefit of hindsight they could see that the European answer was no answer at all. And they reached that conclusion as America rose to world supremacy. The great upheavals of the nineteenth century—the birth of vast labour movements, working class rebellions, popular revolutions, and the growth of strong socialist parties—were met with astonishment and growing suspicion across the Atlantic. Marx had promised that communism would bring about a society where everyone could be what he or she dreamed—creating new roles and experiences and combining them at will—but, desirable as the goal might be, was political revolution really necessary? Would it not be much better if each person pursued an individual dream, an image of perfection, in his or her life and left everyone else alone to do the same?

Europeans and Americans started to diverge in their paths when they discovered radically different solutions to the same shared problem. I hesitate to give it a simple label, but it is a problem all of us are familiar with. As modern society grew in complexity and organization, the role for each person was increasingly specialized. Division of labour dictated that the individual assume his or her place in a gigantic organism. Society would not work if people wanted to do many things at once or if they insisted on experimenting with different possibilities. Instead one made a virtue of conformity, the trained disposition to look for our dedicated role in the vast social organism and be successful at it. By success, of course, was meant collective success—think of the way a single figure for economic growth becomes the core of public policy. The fact that we were all parts of the same organism, cogs of the same machine, ensured a very high level of coherence and uniformity. Functionally distinct, we might never acquire the independence from which genuine individuality could grow. What the collective determined as good and proper we took as good and proper—and the collective, of course, could never agree on anything but an average. "It is real hard to be free," the Jack Nicholson character in *Easy Rider* says, "when you are bought and sold in the marketplace."

Modern man experienced these conditions as a prison, one all the more intolerable as it seemed to be the only prison left. Religion, tradition, the privileges of birth, and the tragedies of disease had largely been eliminated. In their place, society emerged as the great immovable power to which one must submit—or be damned. Europeans and Americans faced the same problem in an equally desperate and urgent manner, but they inclined to different and opposite solutions. While Europeans concluded that society had to be rebuilt on better foundations, Americans despaired of the task—which seemed to them to sink the individual into deeper and deeper forms of social control—and opted to look for ways in which one might simply escape from reality rather than embark on the risky venture to change it.

It was a solution with deep roots in American history. When the economist Werner Sombart tried to determine why the American working class could have become the "peaceful citizens that they are"—why, in brief, socialism had never taken root in the United States—he found the main cause in the peculiar ability that American capitalism had shown to offer workers "an escape from the orbit of the capitalist economy." The escape was this: workers with sound limbs, the adventurous, the rebellious, could turn themselves into independent farmers almost as they wished by colonizing empty land. "Go West, my boy." All throughout the nineteenth century, deep economic crises had often precipitated the growth of radical movements. In Chicago anarchism raised its head. The following of the Knights of Labor exploded in numbers and reached almost one million members in 1886. Each time the force of the storm was broken because those suffering most grievously from what Sombart calls "the nexus of capitalist organization" could leave for the free land in the West and did so in massive numbers. More important than leaving, though, was knowing that you could leave: "The mere knowledge that he could become a free farmer at any time could not but make the American worker feel secure and content, a state of mind that is unknown to his European counterpart. One tolerates any oppressive situation more easily if one lives under the illusion of being able to withdraw from it if really forced to."[20] Sombart thought that in the new century this escape route would disappear. He could not imagine that many more—the infinite roads of the imagination from Kerouac and Updike's *Rabbit* and Richard Yates to *Fear and Loathing in Las Vegas* and *Fight Club*—would replace the old West.

Once Europe got back on its feet—with its major economies experiencing three decades of fast growth and the European project healing past divisions—differences between the two sides of the transatlantic alliance began to emerge. In America a new generation of diplomats and politicians was arriving on the scene, the first to have grown up and succeeded in a world no longer marked by European power and overtly racial categories. While Dean Acheson was secretary of state, he visited Europe at least eleven times but claimed to be too busy to make even a single trip to East Asia.[21] The baby-boomers would grow up in a different world, a fact amply illustrated by the three American presidents coming from that cohort: Clinton, Dubya, Trump.

Across the Atlantic, de Gaulle gave voice to the European urge to liberate the continent from American hegemony. In August 1962 he explained to Alain Peyrefitte—a long-term confidant and spokesperson, and his minister of information in the French government at the time—what Europe was all about: "What is the point of Europe? The point is that one is not dominated by either the Russians or the Americans." But even de Gaulle is ambiguous on the point that I consider the most critical and difficult. Was the question to be decided between the two sides of the transatlantic community about the relative distribution of power or did it go deeper than that? Could it be addressed by a new grand bargain by which Europeans acquired managing rights in the common transatlantic project or was it rooted in fundamental differences of values and outlook?

The question was posed with renewed vigour after the collapse of communism. The disappearance of the common enemy which so often had provided the glue holding Europe and America together now raised the fear—or the hope—that the great alliance might be coming to an end. The United States was quick to respond to the new conditions. Before the Berlin Wall had come down, President George Bush stated: "The United States is and will remain a European power." He soon explained what the thesis meant in practice: the United States would maintain a significant military presence in Europe. Both Bush and Secretary of State James Baker seemed to have in mind earlier lessons. The United States had triumphed in the Cold War, but the work of building a sustainable new European political order had only just begun. As a new age of talks and agreements between West and East opened up, Nato was seen as the forum where Western nations would develop a collective position and a common strategy on the "new security architecture".

The disappearance of the Soviet Union offered an opportunity to redefine the transatlantic community in terms of shared values and goals rather than a shared enemy. Since obstacles would always be present in some form, a permanent framework capable of furthering the values of the liberal democratic world would be needed. Writing in 1995, in the wake of the Balkan wars, Richard Holbrooke singled out the threat of historical resentments and territorial or ethnic disputes as the new "great problems". Only the adoption of Western democratic ideals for all of Europe could provide stability. In this new world, Bosnia was as great a threat to the West as the Soviet Union before its fall. "The West must expand to central Europe as fast as possible in fact as well as in spirit, and the United States is ready to lead the way." If it wanted to survive, the transatlantic community would have to become more explicitly rooted in common ideals and committed to their expansion, even as Europe—now equally prosperous—played a larger role.[22] By the end of the Cold War, Europeans had developed their own vision of the world, and the creation of a single market with regulatory power gave them a new tool with which to pursue it. Increasingly their strategic priority was the European project rather than a much vaguer Western identity. Building a united Europe took precedence over building a united West.

In the face of a widening Atlantic in respect of strategy and tactics, a possible solution was to go back to fundamentals, the ideals bridging different strategic cultures. Holbrooke may have hoped for a permanent arrangement of this kind, but in the years ahead deep disagreements would emerge between Europe and the United States and in some cases between different European countries. Two moments stand out: the debate on whether or not to invade Iraq and the presidency of Donald Trump. They were disagreements not about policy but about the meaning of the "Western democratic ideals" that Holbrooke took for granted.

When he turned to what drew Americans and Europeans apart during the Iraq War, Robert Kagan famously argued that they had developed different and even opposite views on power politics. America is from Mars, Europe from Venus. Europe saw the use of military power as an implicit recognition of failure and a return to the same vision of world politics that had brought the continent so much misery. The current European emphasis on international law and multilateralism may seem like a rejection of the European past, but there is a deeper continuity. What unites European history is the search for a new political order. European concerns are primarily aimed at challenges such as ethnic conflict, migration, education, poverty and environmental degradation—deep structural causes of international conflict calling for sustained and organized solutions. The effort to address the contradictions inherent in international conflict appeals to the European mind of today as much as it did one or two centuries ago. Having transformed the direction of European history and created a successful experiment in the transcendence of power politics through common institutions, Europeans now hope to convert the whole world to the same method. Iraq, North Korea, Iran, Libya: "These states may be dangerous and unpleasant, and even, if simplistic Americans insist, evil. But Germany was evil once, too." Might not the European approach work again, as it did in Europe?[23]

From an American perspective, those debates seem increasingly arcane. Americans no longer see the world as a reflection of enduring political truths but as an arena for power politics. In fact, the less the world approaches an ideal state the greater will be the threats and opportunities it offers as prompts for action. Americans see the world as an action movie, Europeans as a documentary.

Kagan wrote: "Americans are quicker to acknowledge the existence of threats, even to perceive them where others may not see any, because they can conceive of doing something to meet those threats."[24] It is a curious formulation, almost suggesting that the whole point of the exercise is to be able to do something, and that one works back from the desired actions to the threats that may provide them with logic and force. Reading his 2003 best-seller *Of Paradise and Power* with the benefit of hindsight is a bemusing experience. Kagan considers the European reluctance to support the Iraq War and wonders what is behind the concern with the unnecessary loss of life or the destabilization of the Middle East. Surely, he suggests, no one could be genuinely worried about that.[25]

Most remarkably, Kagan has now written a new book in which he takes the opposite view. Before, it was the Europeans who, with their reluctance to act, endangered the existing world order and the Americans, willing to act alone, who stood as defenders of the faith. After Trump, the willingness to act unilaterally has become the main threat to the liberal order. Trump wants victories over rivals and allies alike, and seems agnostic on the method to obtain them. The result, according to Kagan, is that "the United States starts to look more like a rogue superpower than a nation defending any order of any kind. To the degree that this impression takes hold, it will sap the liberal order of what remains of its confidence and cohesion, and just at the moment that Russia and China are contemplating how far to go in challenging it."[26] The rebellion against the West, which two decades ago was the private project of rogue states, has taken over the United States. "The jungle grows in America, too." In brief, the old Kagan used to say that the world was full of rogue states and only America could stop them. The new Kagan says America is now a rogue state and only America can stop it. To sustain the liberal order "requires enlightenment, a degree of generosity, a belief in the universalism of rights, and, yes, a measure of cosmo-politanism that Americans have not lately been displaying."[27] But is it surprising that a superpower used to going its own way should end up departing from the consensus of norms and institutions holding it back? Was it really plausible to think that the United States, free of all other constraints, would continue to accept the limitations of the liberal order?

The collective sense in Washington—and it is by no means limited to Trump—is that Western idealism has become unmanageable. From the left comes the admonition against trying to export a Western model to the rest of the world, often by means of war. On the right, the desire for a world where the United States can free itself from the shackles of a rules-based order and genuinely exercise its rights as the most powerful country in the world exerts a greater and greater pull. Even those of a more cautious and objective temperament, who note that a liberal world order would no doubt be in America's interest, wonder if there really is such a thing. Mahatma Gandhi, on being asked, "What do you think of Western civilization?" was reported to have answered, "I think it would be a good idea." Many liberals today nod their assent. A liberal world order would be a good idea, but what we have today is a shadow play: the United States accepts the restrictions implied by a rules-based order while China, Russia and Iran break all the rules. In such a game, the player who voluntarily ties his own hands is destined to lose. No surprise that many in Washington want to put an end to what they see as a charade or that others increasingly see the notion of a global liberal order as coterminous with the age of European colonialism. Once the relative distribution of power no longer favours the West—as it overwhelmingly did in the past—the ability to apply and enforce rules on a worldwide scale disappears. The search for a new foreign policy can begin.

Fifteen years ago, in the wake of the Iraq invasion, the historian Niall Ferguson wrote a provocative book arguing that a liberal and benevolent American empire might be just what the world needs—as Bertrand Russell had already noted, an open global order may need a common enforcing power—and expressing his puzzlement that, with its vast resources of power and wealth, the United States so often struggled to impose its will beyond its borders. Ferguson was convinced that the problem was the "absence of a will to power", an "imperial cast of mind", and suggested that vacuum might never be filled. Properly understood, Americans have always been in denial about their imperial power.[28]

Indeed, the limits to American power have only grown since Iraq and seem increasingly connected to the worldwide diffusion of technological power and the growth of rival economic powers and ideological models. The age of global empires may turn out to have been strictly confined in time, dependent on imbalances of technology and knowledge of an inexorably transitory character.

"Next to Himmler, even Babbitt began to look good." The character in the eponymous novel by Sinclair Lewis—the first writer from the United States to receive the Nobel—has always been interpreted and denounced as the image of the soulless American. Everything about this real-estate agent in a typical mid-size Midwestern city during the Roaring Twenties seems to be standard: a standard home, standard home appliances, a standard daily routine, and a standard wife towards whom he has no genuine feelings. Babbitt has no idea what he desires from life, so he has no choice but to desire what others around him desire. They do the same. And it is a good thing everyone is trying to keep up with everyone else. As Babbitt muses, it forces them to "produce—produce—produce!"

The first few chapters of the novel pose acutely the problem of how a novel can be written about someone like Babbitt or about a place like Zenith. The narrative mimics the same empty routine being repeated all over the city. The only things with a soul seem to be the consumer goods that Babbitt effuses about—his symbols of truth and beauty—from the moment he is woken up by a modern first-class alarm clock. Just as the Presbyterian

Church determined his religious beliefs and the Republican Party decided his political views, so the large national advertising companies fixed his very individuality, his most treasured tastes and preferences. All went well.

The novel comes alive when Babbitt has a crisis of conscience. One day it suddenly comes to him that life as he practised it was futile. He did not after all get much pleasure making money, and what in the end was the point of having children so that they in turn could have children who would rear children? A way to postpone the question of what life is for until the next generation. He starts to regard his life as hopelessly mechanical: mechanical business. mechanical religion, mechanical golf and mechanical conversation. "Oh, he wanted to be one of these Bohemians you read about! Studio parties. Wild lovely girls who were independent."

For the last hundred pages of the novel, Babbitt is in rebellion, unable to come to terms with a world which, once doubted, becomes absurd. All the while he keeps his distance from political rebels and revolutionaries: those he associates with European politics, where businessmen have no say and the interests of decency and society are trampled on. The problem with socialism is that it takes up too many evenings. He remains a sound businessman, but one who wants to enjoy life before it is too late. The crisis he is going through is, after all, his individual crisis. It never crosses his mind that it can be solved by anyone else or that a solution can be rehearsed anywhere but in the course of his life.

The solution he envisages is different from the vain and futile attempt to improve society. Preserve the social and economic fabric in its current form but grant each person the freedom to break with convention in his or her actions. Let a thousand revolutions bloom. One person may look for thrilling sensations in his romantic life while another may prefer to build a career of towering achievement. A business trip or a difficult deal may be reinterpreted as a daring challenge or a perilous adventure. Why should Lenin and his comrades have all the fun? A businessman in Zenith may have an equally exciting life and do it in the knowledge that in the morning—after an all-nighter—he has a job to go back to and no assassins lie in wait to make an attempt on his life. The best of both worlds. Eventually, Babbitt fails, but only because it is too late for him. His project will be taken forward by Ted, his son, to whom he explains the facts of life—not procreation but happiness—at the very end and conclusion of the novel.

Babbitt is arguably the greatest American novel ever written because it depicts in vivid detail the path of American modern society before that path was even intelligible to the vast majority of Americans. That it created a sensation, being equally loved and hated, was in itself revealing of a deep cultural change. Henry James had launched similar attacks against American life, but he had to be careful and subtle. Lewis brought everything out into the open because he could afford to. And he seemed to offer a way out, which James never did.

The need to enhance or embellish reality becomes a vital operating system, and it is precisely this longing that Lewis suggests is the difference between Americans and Europeans. Whether on account of the drabness of daily life in the prairies and the soulless cities of his youth or the relative absence of tradition and the past, he saw Americans of all ages and classes engaged in the pursuit of a private dream. Europe, which began for him as a land of desire, slowly became a fantasy, taking its place in the American psyche among an endless gallery of romantic visions. Against all odds, the generation after *Babbitt* would build its own version of Bohemia, but in contrast to bohemian life in Europe, this was not a project of social and political transformation but an individual escape from the drudgery of social life. Greenwich

Village, where Sinclair Lewis lived and to which he would remain connected, had been born in the years just before 1922, when *Babbitt* was published. One author calls it the "republic of dreams," noting that Greenwich Village in the twenties "explored revolutionary forms in order to express traditional American values." As for Villagers of the forties and fifties, they "luxuriated in almost placid disaffection, the hope of transformation turned into a desire to be left alone."[29]

The image of society that we find in movies such as *Bonnie and Clyde* or *Easy Rider*—the origins of a "new Hollywood" critical of the old studio conventions—is that of a vast, unknown space where individual adventurers are free to create worlds of their own, often gaining sustenance and meaning from the very traditions and structures standing in their way. To be reconciled with society as a field of combat and contradictions and to abandon all plans to improve it might reveal a deeply conservative, even an atavistic, disposition, but I believe it is possible to consider the American mind from a different perspective. Perhaps Americans no longer think of society as a home. Perhaps they regard it as a theme park or an obstacle course; an arena. With characteristic acumen, Tom Wolfe noted the basic difference between America and Europe when he made a lecture tour of Italy. The Italian students he met in 1971 were interested in one question. These were politically active students, members of radical organizations and used to pitched street battles with the police. But theirs were social and political struggles. In their private lives they took fewer liberties, returning home after those battles for dinner with their families and a little television. They wanted to hear from Wolfe how the American youth were actually leaving home and joining others to live by their own rules. "Creating worlds of their own," as Wolfe put it.[30]

Europe, old Europe. Europe still suffers—deeply and personally—from the moral ruins of Auschwitz. We have not yet come to terms with all that it means for us. As the Turkish historian Huri Islamoglu once told me—we were sitting in her apartment overlooking the Bosphorus—it is entirely possible that European politics have been forever ruined by Nazism. After all, if everything about your political instincts and values is organized around the repudiation of Nazism, you are still living in the grip of its ghosts. We wander and search for something, but all we know as a solid truth is that it must be the opposite of Nazism and that any path taking us in other directions is by definition a dangerous one. We have lost the heart to be fully free because we fear making the old mistakes. We condemn all forms of hatred, even those that have been with humankind since its very birth, because in all of them we see Hitler's reflection. We continue to look for the perfect society because it is in this search—in Milton and Machiavelli and Montesquieu—that our world and our civilization were born. But if that search seemed beyond our strength when we put all our strength into it, can it really be successful when we doubt ourselves?

These are still today the most difficult questions for a European. They do not have the same meaning for an American. More than anything else, it is Auschwitz that pulls us apart.

FOUR

As America enjoyed the glories of a postwar boom, its serious, hardworking, sober self suffered a radical transfiguration. Jackson Pollock inaugurated the first genuinely American art and it was a lot more about the gesture, the act of creation, than the finished product. The American penchant for action was combined with intellectual knowingness. The canvas suddenly started to appear to one American painter after another as a stage on which to act rather than a space in which to reproduce or even to transform reality. What was to happen on the canvas was not a picture but an event. The painter had become an actor, and in this transformation the usual catching up with European art forms came to a halt. Americans were playing by a different set of rules.[1]

The gravitas was fading, the centre of gravity shifting away from New England and New York to the dream world of California. By 1955 America could feel pride in a young coterie of writers and artists it might finally call its own. Would anyone ever mistake Jack Kerouac or Elvis Presley for Europeans? It was the year Disneyland opened.

In an essay published in March 1961—and this is the first such claim I have been able to find—the novelist Philip Roth argued that the challenge for the American writer would henceforth be to make reality more plausible or credible. Not to expand real events but to contain them. "It stupefies, it sickens, it infuriates, and finally it is even a kind of embarrassment to one's own meager imagination. The actuality is continually outdoing our talents, and the culture tosses up figures almost daily that are the envy of any novelist." And he gave the example of the famous television debate between Kennedy and Nixon: "All the machinations over make-up, rebuttal time, all the business over whether Mr. Nixon should look at Mr. Kennedy when he replied, or should look away—all of it was so beside the point, so fantastic, so weird and astonishing, that I found myself beginning to wish I had invented it." For two reasons, he added. Firstly, because it was very good as literature. Secondly, if it had been invented, it would not be real, and no one would be forced to live with it. "The daily newspapers then fill one with wonder and awe: is it possible? is it happening?"[2] Television was eating the world.

In a book published the same year, the historian Daniel Boorstin could already warn his contemporaries that "we risk being the first people in history to have been able to make their illusions so vivid, so persuasive, so realistic that they can live in them. We are the most illusioned people on Earth. Yet we dare not become disillusioned, because our illusions are the very house in which we live; they are our news, our heroes, our adventure, our forms of art, our very experience."[3]

Americans have been leading a double life, Norman Mailer suggested in 1960, and American history has moved on two rivers, one visible, the other underground. There has been the history of politics, which is concrete, factual, practical and dull, and also a subterranean river of romantic desires, the dream life of the nation. The springs of this underground river he located in that moment when the frontier was finally conquered and the expansion turned inward, becoming part of an agitated, overexcited, superheated dream life. The romantic possibilities of the old conquest of land turned into a vertical myth, trapped within the skull and shamelessly exploited by the Hollywood film studios. With Kennedy the subterranean river, its violent force, was felt at the surface. When the candidate arrived at the Democratic convention—in Los Angeles, naturally—Mailer detected a certain uneasiness at what was about to happen. "America's politics would now be also America's favorite movie, America's first soap opera, America's best-seller." But everything stayed within limits—for the time being. Kennedy might look like a movie star, his manner rich and his gestures strong and quick, but his public mind, his ideas, were conventional. In 1960 the law of political life was still that only a conventional mind could win an election.[4]

The Cold War, which at first may have been fought by sober and industrious professionals, had acquired its own forms of unreality. The Sputnik launch by the Soviet Union in 1957 moved at least an element of the planetary battle for dominance to outer space, where imagination ruled supreme. The United States concluded from the episode that the victor in the struggle for the future might well be the side with the most creative imagination. It no longer sufficed to be ahead; the contestants had to ensure that they appeared to be ahead. Gore Vidal reports a conversation he once had with Kennedy after he came back from the famous Vienna conference with Khrushchev. Vidal was full of his usual liberal ideas, arguing that the Soviets posed no threat to America. According to him, Kennedy felt inclined to agree but then added: "In this kind of politics, it is the appearance of things that matters." It was an occasion for the great novelist to go back to his notion that the only art form the United States had ever created was the television commercial.[5]

Would global public opinion side with the best political regime or might it be feared that, being the child of a growing media culture, it would follow those capable of putting on a bigger and more exciting show? When audiences all over the world tuned in to watch the Apollo moon landing, Americans felt confident in their final victory against the "evil empire", a term Reagan borrowed directly from the movies.

Reality and unreality were increasingly coming together, and Watergate helped bridge most of the remaining distance. It was a symbolic moment, of course. If you could not trust the president to tell you the truth, whom could you trust? And if that president, rather than lying like everyone else, had created a giant system of deception, how could you be sure it was even possible to know the truth?

Nixon looked to many—even at the time—as the sort of presidential character a novelist would create: psychologically conflicted, even tortured, riddled by contradictions, brilliantly farsighted and yet so flawed that his political fate was bound to become the public display of his personal character. The Watergate hearings were the first American political soap opera and the model for all soap operas to come. Contemporary accounts describe the sense of vertigo most American citizens then experienced for the first time. Had they left the real world and entered a fictional drama created by a hidden and evil playwright?

It was not that events were horrible or inconceivable. Those categories have always been part of human and political experience. There was nothing new about the corrupting force of power or the weakness of political institutions. No, what those stunned onlookers saw was what the onlookers at the Los Angeles Democratic convention more than a decade earlier had already sensed, that a new order was claiming human experience as raw material for fiction. Nixon had become a victim of the laws of drama. He was a character in a movie. Little surprise that when *All the President's Men* came out in 1976, Watergate suddenly started to make sense. The movie gave it depth.

There is a famous dramatic principle stating that if a writer or scriptwriter shows us that there is a rifle hanging on the wall, in one of the following scenes it absolutely must go off. And so it was with Watergate. It felt unreal because it so clearly followed the laws of drama. Narrative possibilities were studiously explored and exhausted. Every character played its part and seemed to prepare the way for the following act. Everyone and everything had to find its place within the plot line. When the denouement arrived, it seemed both plausible and awe-inspiring. Watergate was still a classical impeachment, with one episode at a time so you could keep up.[6]

As the Watergate drama unfolded, another equally ponderous—but almost unknown—story was being written just south of San Francisco. These were the years Silicon Valley became what it still is today, a fantasy land where engineering talent and capital come together to power the serious project of creating new worlds out of nothing. In 1972 one of the eight men who had formed the Silicon Valley pioneer Fairchild Semiconductor founded the venture capital firm Kleiner Perkins. In the same year, a former Fairchild sales executive founded Sequoia Capital. Kleiner Perkins and Sequoia would become as intrinsic to Silicon Valley as the entrepreneurs themselves. They were "the equivalent of the grand Hollywood studios, with the entrepreneurs analogous to actors, directors, and producers." It was also the year a new company named Atari created Pong, one of the very first video games, and Hewlett-Packard launched the first scientific pocket calculator, announcing in the owner's manual: "We thought you'd like to have something only fictional heroes like James Bond, Walter Mitty or Dick Tracy are supposed to own." One Atari ad in 1974 read simply, "Have Fun, Make Money." The day the ad ran, an eighteen-year-old who had grown up in nearby Cupertino showed up at the front desk of the game maker. He refused to leave without a job and was eventually hired, even though he was a dropout from the literary Reed College with no formal engineering background. His name was Steve Jobs.[7]

For the next four decades, American politics and American business would never cease approaching the ideal point where they would be indistinguishable from Hollywood. Reagan said that politics was just like show business. He came from Hollywood and understood better than anyone that the country's life needed new myths. He often explained to his interlocutors that he would never understand how anyone could be president without having first been an actor. It is an interesting sentence, even if Reagan did not mean it in full seriousness. On some obvious level, he did mean it. Movies were a source of endless material for speeches and impromptu comments. Some of Reagan's most inspired moments happened once he let his prodigious memory of cinema quotes dictate what he said. Movies give you emotional intelligence and prepare you for crises. After all, every movie is about a crisis of some kind. He loved *War Games*, in which a teenage hacker inadvertently sets off the nuclear codes, and was impressed by *Firefox*, in which Clint Eastwood is recruited to steal a Soviet fighter jet controlled by telepathy. Both would inspire government programmes and help propel a revolution in military affairs. But movies offered a promise of peace as well. Reagan told Gorbachev that only an extraterrestrial invasion could trump national differences and Cold War rivalry, a proposal that—as National Security Advisor General Colin Powell immediately recognized—had been inspired by the 1951 movie *The Day the Earth Stood Still*.[8]

After his movie career was effectively over, Reagan starred in what was television's first reality show, opening his new ranch-style house to the public in order to exhibit—together with Nancy and Patti—all the latest domestic gadgets with which General Electric had equipped it. The nightly reel made him an instant celebrity. Unknown to the viewers, it would eventually make him president.

What Reagan opposed was the exhausted medium of liberalism and its logic of destruction. He wanted Americans to live more like movie characters, lost in many different identities and relaxed about their ultimate truth or meaning. Many have noticed that his critical ideological tenets had a certain levity, even frivolity. He never followed through with what the religious right interpreted as specific promises on abortion and other matters. He was never able to reduce the size of the welfare state or reform social security. But was Reagan interested in material changes of this kind? He succeeded without them by endowing the personal mythologies of business and family values with the same power of those translucent images which the moviegoer replays in his mind as he leaves the theatre, holding the promise of a more exciting and more beautiful life.

To say that Reagan's policies were contradictory—that, for example, they tried to promote traditional values while unfettering forms of financial capitalism that were ill at ease with a traditional way of life—is to miss the point. They were as contradictory as two Hollywood movies that might present different and opposite human types—a nun and a libertine, for example. All human possibilities may be simultaneously pursued. None can claim a special status. None is true if by true we mean true in isolation. They are equally interesting and equally worth pursuing. As Jules Feiffer once said, when addressing Reagan's defence of religious creationism: "If Reagan had played Darwin in a movie, he would believe in evolution."

As religion, business, leisure and career—all the spheres of private life—became raw material for fiction, the same pressures were about to conquer the world of politics. If Nixon became a victim of the laws of drama, every president after him came into office with one main goal in mind: to shape the narrative rather than be shaped by it. Here too Reagan was an innovator, introducing a new way of thinking about communications. His team, led by a young David Gergen, deliberately set out to "think like a television producer." If White House politics is an ongoing story about political power and how it is exercised, then the Reagan administration would combine the roles of actor and scriptwriter. Which came first? One suspects the scriptwriter, although this was still a far shot from the world of Bill Clinton—when coverage of the White House was almost always coverage of how Clinton tried to control the narrative and the news was more often than not about the news. While Reagan was an actor playing the role of president, Clinton was an actor playing a new and different role every day. As Michael Kelly wrote, his face approached the state of a screen upon which played a loop of expressions: the lip biting, the lowered eyes of humility, the open-mouth grin of joy. "Clinton means what he says when he says it, but tomorrow he will mean what he says when he says the opposite."[9]

The surreal saga of O.J. Simpson in 1994, like the Lewinsky story a few years later, was emblematic of the Clinton years, a revolutionary time when reality kept surpassing fiction at its own game. The Simpson case had everything. The reversal of fortune suffered by a successful man, the typical car chase of an action movie, and the courtroom drama of a classic whodunnit. Lewinsky was a story about nothing, inspired by light sitcoms such as *Seinfeld*—and *Seinfeld*'s last episode was aired during the height of the scandal. Imagine a novel with this for a first paragraph: "In November 1997, Monica Lewinsky told her confidante and supposed friend, Linda Tripp, that she had in her possession a blue Gap dress that still bore the semen stain that resulted from her administering oral sex to President Clinton in February of that year." It felt unreal not because it dealt with extraordinary events, but because nothing really happened—for weeks and weeks—and yet it kept happening. The two scandals were distinctive in their ability to suggest to European audiences that the United States was no longer comprehensible.

It is a futile endeavour to try to pinpoint when things changed in America. They changed slowly, they are still changing, and no change can be complete until it is correctly perceived and affirmed by human consciousness. What we do detect without much effort is a difference in gradient and direction. European liberalism was a force of liberation. It was the liberal state that rescued the youth from family tradition, women from patriarchy, the individual from group rules, the craftsman from guild tyranny. For classical liberalism, the self is defined by its capacity to choose. Detached from every value and goal, it prizes aloofness, coolness, disenchantment. There is nothing above to which it may owe loyalty or devotion.

The "coolness" aesthetic—the first fully modern aesthetic—was originally expressive of a stubborn lack of conformity: being cool was to say what one wanted, wear what one pleased, act always without fear of consequences, especially social consequences. But the word has changed, perhaps everywhere English is spoken—and rather dramatically in America. Impassive, aloof, amused, nonchalant, the cool person—so it used to be—is dismissive of the idea of objective meaning. He believes in himself or she believes in herself. In a cold, dark universe, the individual alone is able to endow things with meaning. There is no point in getting too excited or to trust in anything beyond our own will and action.

That was the old meaning of the word. It still survives. In Europe it remains popular—it was a form of indoctrination for young Europeans my age—but in America it has changed beyond recognition. When we say that something is cool we now mean it is "interesting" or "exciting"; something capable of attracting our interest. Humphrey Bogart was cool. Now cool is, say, a clown riding a bicycle upside down. Quite a change. The shift from the older to the new meaning typifies the radical change from the classical American sensibility—indistinguishable from the European sensibility that shaped the cool aesthetic from the British stiff upper lip to French existentialism—to modern

America. I propose to look at two great American novels, written a lifespan apart, as a way to introduce that shift: from the disenchantment to the re-enchantment of the world.

In the 1925 novel *The Great Gatsby*—the culmination of the European way of life in America—the story is that of the lonely individual struggling against the forces of convention as he pursues his personal vision of happiness. That vision was bound to be defeated because no individual can stand up to the social whole and because only failure can certify that his or her vision was purely personal and subjective, divorced from the world of realities the moment it was first conceived. Gatsby is presented as being better than everyone else, "worth more than the whole bunch put together", because of his secret life, the "incorruptible dream" concealed within; but he is also a model of failure and inaction, intensely incapable of fighting for that distant dream— a green light at the end of a dock marking the house belonging to his beloved Daisy—which he starts to doubt at the very moment it is close to realization. I could never become very interested in Gatsby because—for all its lyricism and formal perfection—it read like a European novel, imported from Europe a few decades after the original product became common there.

In *Infinite Jest*, the sprawling 1996 novel by David Foster Wallace, the real story is the story itself. The struggle is that of the story to develop and cohere into a finished book. The author sets out the conflict in terms of the very largesse of the story's range, swept across endless characters and topics, whose inclusion can only be justified or motivated by the story as a whole. At one point the narrator makes a connection between certain fractal curvature theories and the game of tennis. There is a terrorist group and a North American superstate, calendar years sponsored by corporations, and a movie so funny it can kill you. These elements are rather miraculously brought together in an overarching plot. By the end of the book we know the story, the story of the book we have just read.

FOUR

What the most recent American literature does is to take this idea to its logical conclusion; to democratize it, in a way. Novelists are irresistibly drawn to stories of characters that have in themselves some of the traits of a novelist. That is true today as it was a hundred years ago. But the characters giving life to recent American novels—by Jeffrey Eugenides, for example—look like postmodern writers. They lead their lives as creators anxious about the coherence of their plots and the meaning of their experiences. The characters in *The Marriage Plot* by Eugenides alternate between writer's block—they wander about unsure of what to do next—and bursts of sudden creativity when their life stories take interesting turns. They also worry that they have simply ruined their lives in a way that makes it sound as if they are worried those lives would never find an audience or that the audience will merely laugh at something rather too comic or Shakespearean. The title of the novel is, of course, a reference to novel-writing, just as *Gravity's Rainbow*, Thomas Pynchon's greatest novel, referred to the arc of narrative, akin to a rainbow.

Notice how everything can find a place in this world of stories. In *The Marriage Plot* some characters struggle to be libertines, others want to be saints or romantic heroines or giants of science. It hardly matters. One can build a great story with all kinds of material. None of the characters takes religion or sex or science very seriously. They build stories using what they can find. They live at some distance from the goals of life, but they are careful not to smash them because if they did they would become like Gatsby—like the existential hero of every Camus or Sartre novel—with nothing to live for. The characters in Eugenides' books do not want to be liberated from their emotions but to have their importance confirmed. They want to be judged as scriptwriters. At a young age they felt they could be characters in a story, and growing up means accepting that they will have to write it themselves. Even the clothes they wear are chosen in accordance with the role they expect to play. Ultimately they want to become bestselling authors of their own lives or, in a word, they want to be famous.

What is remarkable about the most recent American fiction is that it manages to be fixated on literary gimmicks, metafictional strategies and ironic distance while remaining entirely realistic. After all, the human realities it depicts are themselves thoroughly consumed by those gimmicks, strategies and distance.

The classical American hero rises up against convention and tradition in the search for absolute freedom. The modern American hero accepts all the experiences of human life, but transforms them into stories. The individual search is now a search for meaning.

That one could have arrived at the new ideal from the old one is not a random development or even very difficult to explain. On the one hand, the unmasking of the bourgeois belief in objective reality has been so fully accomplished in America that any meaningful struggle against reality has become absurd. Why would the individual continue to battle the world of social institutions and conventions when this world has so obviously lost all authority? And where can we expect to find that hidden substratum of the self, freed from every cultural influence of determination? The modern European project would necessarily mean that every person anywhere in space or time would be identical and equivalent to everyone else. No such mythical creature has ever been found, not even in America. Not Gatsby, surely.

Moreover, the new ideal asks much less of human beings in their approach to life. Rather than being confined to the loneliness of their individual selves, they could inhabit a rich social world of experience and exploration. And rather than dwelling on thoughts and doubts, they could inhabit a world of stories, full of suspense and surprise, a world replenished with the ghosts of the past. Most people, if offered the choice, would prefer to live in Disneyland than in the sanatorium high up in the Swiss Alps where Thomas Mann placed his fable of the European soul.

The difference is well captured by the contrasting way Americans and Europeans experience spectator sports. In Europe, sports are for the most part an escape or, better put, a reverse escape: having flown from community and meaning and fate, Europeans see in sports—in the inescapable reality of their team attachments—a return to the enchanted world of the past where fate is to a great extent beyond our control. For Americans, sports are an intensification of experience. They portray life in ideal form, with its perfect stories of overcoming, excess, world-historical achievement and, generally speaking, the sense of miracle.

And so, looked at from the distant future, it suddenly appears that Americans did not originally leave Europe in search of freedom of worship or freedom from hierarchy or the overbearing power of the state: mastery, kingship, fatherhood; kings and bishops and popes. No, they left Europe to escape the vanishingly small world of European experience, the European self enclosed within the limits of its own mind. They sailed to America to get away from themselves. They wanted to break out into a wider world. Red pill or blue pill?

When I studied in the United States, my first genuine impression of America was those college students who, without drinking, shouted as if drunk and, not even happy, laughed as if enraptured. Why would they act like this? Because, precisely, they were acting. They were actors trying to live up to their role of drunk college students.

Tyler Cowen asks somewhere why Americans are so loud. This seems to be a generally accepted fact, although I am not aware of any scientific studies confirming it. Cowen does not dispute it and lists a number of reasons that could help explain it. It might be, for example, that Americans command a broader personal space and, keeping more distance, they need to speak louder to be understood. Or it may be that in a nation of immigrants language proficiency is often poor and needs to be compensated by volume. Finally, social status may be a variable. Higher-status people tend to talk in hushed tones, since they command attention by their status alone, and their habits quite literally set the tone for society as a whole. It may be that, deprived of a natural aristocracy, Americans have always needed to speak louder.

I am not convinced by any of these hypotheses. So here is my suggestion. Typically an American in a job interview is not content to show he is qualified. He wants to show he knows how to do a job interview: flawlessly, without noise, without hesitation, like an actor on stage. And typically an American having some drinks in a bar does not simply want to have some fun. She wants to show she knows how to have fun: with commitment, enthusiasm and earnestness.

My hypothesis is that American life continuously emphasizes its own artificiality in a way that reminds participants that, deep down, they are experiencing a story. The American way of life is consciously about language, storytelling, plot and form, and is meant to draw attention to its status as fiction. This element may range from strongly scripted structures of daily life—the prom dance, retirement in Florida—to the blurring of lines between fact and fiction, with life being subject to narrative evaluation. "Would this work in a book or television series" is a question that makes more and more sense when interrogating specific ideals of individual conduct or even political success.

The weak hold of traditional social structures, the ideal of invention and creativity, the love of modern technology—these were all traits that America inherited from European modernity and that prepared it for its final turn towards fictional structures. Hollywood, Disneyland and Vegas were perhaps the earliest manifestations of this ideal, but it is only recently that artificiality invaded all spheres of life and society, breaking the barrier between fact and fiction. As Kurt Andersen puts it, "the American experiment, the original embodiment of the great Enlightenment idea of intellectual freedom, every individual free to believe anything she wishes, has metastasized out of control."[10] In America today, reality is experienced through the fictionalized enactment of its opposite. It is now possible for the American president to announce the resumption of sanctions against Iran by means of a meme depicting him as a *Game of Thrones* character: "Sanctions Are Coming."

All these American plots are really about stories, they are stories of stories, attempts to create compelling and exciting life stories. Their protagonists are without exception storytellers and their human problems are technical problems of storytelling.

There is a question worth raising at this point, although it is one we shall often return to. A society of stories, if it wants to live up to its ideal, cannot be a society of fully resolved conflicts and contradictions. Yes, a weekend in Vegas may well promise to deliver one of those "what happens in Vegas" stories to take home to your friends, but the potential for trouble is as limitless as the stories. Trouble and fiction are connected, violence is locked with creativity. Reduce the constraints on individual desire and satisfaction, eliminate danger and suffering, build the world upon eternal love, banish all forms of hatred and violence—and you may end up with very weak stories and very poor material on which to build them. Could *Romeo and Juliet* take place in a liberal society where class divisions and family ties have been weakened? Of course not. Other stories would be possible, no doubt, but if progress eliminates all forms of conflict, then we have a problem on our hands. In that classic American form, the Western, the town does not provide a home for the cowboy—it is not the safe and conveniently anonymous field of experience a European city promises the romantic *flaneur*—but a hostile place, full of conflict and danger.[11]

Even in a novelist so blatantly natural and direct in his approach as Jonathan Franzen, fantasy is everywhere. A character struggles to express his love for his wife or to save his marriage, and he does this as a writer struggling to find a compelling way to express love or to develop the story in a way that most readers will find plausible. But these characters are not literary characters in the sense that they might be found on the pages of a novel. They are literary while existing in the world around us because the world is now made of books, movies and television series. They are plausible, natural, obvious. Their stories are powerfully real, more real perhaps than what reality used to be. A love story in the world of realities is always imperfect, fuzzy, indistinct. It develops without conviction because no one is exploring the storytelling possibilities to the fullest. But when a love story is experienced as a story, then it acquires a fullness—but also a kind of pharmacological purity—that would always evade the original. The copy surpasses the original.

The childhood stories lived out in real time and space in Disneyland would eventually become the model for stories lived out everywhere. Today everything looks like Disneyland. Life imitates fiction and fiction gives up on trying to measure up. Or, to put it differently, today the fantasy has become more important than reality because reality strives to organize itself according to the fantasy. On Wall Street everything strives to approach the ideal offered by *Wall Street*, the movie. On campus a myriad of campus movies help make sense of events. The romantic comedy has invaded every conversation rehearsed on first dates all over town. And the White House? The White House is either *House of Cards* or *West Wing*, depending on which party is currently in power.

That is why it fundamentally misses the point to compare Donald Trump to other celebrities and even entertainers in the past who embraced a political career. Berlusconi or Schwarzenegger used their fame and the technics of entertainment to appear as more genuine and more appealing politicians than they really were. They made an effort to become politicians or at least to project the image of a politician. Trump is the opposite. As Stephen Duncombe puts it, he does not use the tricks of enter-tainment to appear a better politician, he uses politics as a better stage for his performance as an entertainer—a paradigm shift, a Copernican turn. When asked if he would accept the results of the election, Trump ended the final presidential debate with a classic cliffhanger: "I will keep you in suspense."[12] Discussing possible sanctions against Turkey, he tweeted in October 2019: "Treasury is ready to go, additional legislation may be sought. There is great consensus on this. Turkey has asked that it not be done. Stay tuned!" More dramatically, he explained during a rally in Minneapolis the same month: "That was one of the greatest nights in the history of television. It was one of the highest rated evenings in the history of television." As Jonathan Chait of *New York Magazine* commented in amazement, the president of the United States thinks of his own election as a show that he watched on television.[13]

At present, of course, and for the past few years, there is one particular movie plot organizing Washington politics: *The Manchurian Candidate*. Produced at the height of the Cold War and based on the 1959 Richard Condon novel, it must have been intended—and perceived—as the deliberate exploration of an extreme narrative possibility. The genre of spy thrillers had accustomed viewers to a thrilling game of identity: was a spy really working for the other side or was he a double agent pre-tending to do so in order to better penetrate the enemy's defences or to pass on carefully selected disinformation? *The Manchurian Candidate* suggested a variation. The secret agent it presents us with is a saboteur rather than a spy, but this is a saboteur of a particular kind. Shaw is a war hero just returned from Korea. His mother has remarried. We slowly learn that she is in fact working for the Russians and her husband is a United States senator with even higher ambitions. As for Shaw, one of the initial scenes shows us how he was captured in the jungle and then brainwashed by Russian scientists from the Pavlov Institute in Moscow. A specific visual trigger drives him into a state of hypnosis during which he comes to resemble a human robot, an unconscious sleeper agent. He is above all suspicion, but of course even his heroic feats in Korea were manufactured by his captors, who have also brainwashed the men in his platoon into recommending him for a Medal of Honor.

Now, the story of Donald Trump and Russia is not exactly the same but only because it far exceeds *The Manchurian Candidate* in narrative inventiveness. Interestingly, the way it has developed and expanded is similar to the way in which a scriptwriter might have developed a script. There were some initial elements without which no one could have become interested in the concept in the first place: the fact of Russian interference in the presidential election, notably the hacking and disseminating of emails detrimental to Hillary Clinton, an unusual level of sympathy expressed by Donald Trump towards Russia and President Vladimir Putin, and, finally, the existence of contacts during the campaign between members of the Trump campaign and different Russian characters, more or less close to or having access to the Kremlin. A dossier circulated at the time provided the missing link. Why did Trump seem to harbour such warm feelings towards Putin? It must be because he is in fact controlled by Putin, not through hypnosis but by *kompromat*, a Russian word quickly learned by journalists and commentators. He was being blackmailed by the Kremlin, which at some point in the past came in possession of compromising information about the American president, and could be expected to be called into action when his controllers saw the best opportunity to tip the scales of world power in their favour.

The facts of the matter are that a plot too incredible to be offered as fiction is now being seriously discussed and contemplated as reality. How has this happened? It does not help to say that the plot may in fact be real. If it happened to be real in all its incredible details, it would not thereby stop being fundamentally implausible. Fiction would not lose its character by taking over reality.

In any event, the Russia collusion story is far from the only example of how Trump symbolizes a new way to look at reality—or to avert your gaze from reality. How did he get elected in the first place? We all remember how the possibility was openly laughed at by every expert, and not long before it became reality. But in a world where voters want to be entertained, the story was not devoid of appeal. A property developer who lived his life perfecting an image of boisterous vulgarity, could he actually win the highest political office in the country? Perhaps not, but as a story it could work. It was easy to imagine a large audience tuning in every evening to watch a political series with exactly that plot. At this point something interesting happens because an audience interested in a fictional plot is by definition interested in seeing the next twists and even in carrying it to the end. The psychological urge to see what happens next and even to see a story through to the end seemed already at play in the election of Barack Obama eight years earlier. Viewers will not abandon a good storyline before the end, provided it is able to sustain their interest. As for voters, perhaps they are now better understood as viewers than as citizens or consumers, categories once used but no longer apt.

Trump has a certain awareness of these fundamental facts. I mentioned already how he tweeted the announcement of new sanctions against Iran in the garb of a *Game of Thrones* meme portraying himself as Jon Snow. But that is not all. A few weeks later a photo of a cabinet meeting showed he had actually had the meme printed out as a movie poster, presumably to distribute to cabinet secretaries. Some of the most memorable moments of his presidency seem like short clips from a movie or television series. There was the moment when Trump was joined by Egyptian President Sisi and Saudi King Salman to touch a mysterious crystal orb. As James Parker of *The Atlantic* put it, "the orb was a crystal ball, a node of freemasonry, a concentration of diabolic energy, and the three kings were its slaves. Hydra, the Illuminati, Saruman the White." Then there was the time when he talked privately about fortifying a border wall with a water-filled trench, stocked with snakes or alligators, prompting aides to seek a cost estimate. Or the time he examined documents detailing North Korean ballistic missile capabilities with Japanese Prime Minister Abe while sitting on the patio of his exclusive club, Mar-a-Lago. Smartphone flashlights had to be used to read the top secret papers in the dark. Then he tried to persuade North Korea's dictator to abandon his weapons with a faux movie trailer and, later, tweeted a message announcing a surprise encounter at the demilitarized zone, proudly walking across the border with North Korea with the express purpose of becoming the first American president to do so. In the summer of 2019 he surpassed himself by announcing an interest in buying Greenland from Denmark. When a prosaic and boring Danish prime minister called the idea "absurd", he promptly called off his imminent visit to the country. After the commando raid that led to the death of Islamic State leader Baghdadi, Trump described his last moments in lurid detail ("He died like a dog, he died like a coward, he was whimpering, screaming and crying."). Watching the raid was like a movie, the president added. And so on and so forth.

There are even reports that Trump filled a number of his senior positions by thinking how he would cast a blockbuster television series. Chris Christie, the voluminous former governor of New Jersey, never stood a chance. John Bolton lost the chance to become national security advisor at the beginning of the presidency because Trump was still unconvinced by his moustache. He just did not look the part.[14] Why did he pick James "Mad Dog" Mattis, someone he disagreed with on almost everything, as his first secretary of defense? Because Mattis looked the part: the grids of medals on his chest, the epaulettes and, above all, *that* nickname. The symbol of reality has overcome and replaced reality.[15]

Think of society as the stage where multiple stories and plot lines compete for attention. Some of them are personal stories and follow the rhythms of an individual life. Others are business plans whose appeal to venture capitalists is that they evolve from an idea into a project whose realization will change the world in small and not so small ways. More strangely still—but it was perhaps to be expected—when citizens choose their political leaders, they look to people with recognizable abilities as scriptwriters. The love of unreality may be the most-needed trait in a political leader, who is called upon to move in that higher realm, to avoid the shoals of reality and be guided in his or her decisions by the "interesting" rather than the "true".

In an essay published in 2005, the late Tony Judt addressed the myth that Europe and America are converging on a single Western model of late capitalism. After Trump, his words sound all the more compelling. For Judt—he is really confronting the Tocqueville myth—"America and Europe are not way stations on a historical production line, such that Europeans must expect to inherit or replicate the American experience after an appropriate time lag."[16] They are very different places and, more importantly, they may be drifting apart, going in different directions. And Judt is also correct about the traits that Europeans regard as profoundly alien: America's affection for guns and prisons, its marked religiosity, its embrace of the death penalty, the lack of universal health insurance. We shall have to consider where these traits come from, whether they share a common character and what they tell us about the possibility of a distinctive American culture. Europeans, of course, have their own answer to these questions. It is the exact reverse of the Tocqueville myth. By clinging to guns and religion, the United States shows it is relatively more backward than its European cousins. In some fundamental areas America is still a traditional society, with its belief in transcendence and rather primitive ways to enforce justice and deliver public goods. No other country spends so much money on health care and yet American life expectancy keeps falling. There was once the hope that Obama could play the role of great modernizer, a Mustafa Kemal from the South Side of Chicago. He did accuse his countrymen of clinging to guns and religion. Europeans hoped he could convince them to let go of those ties.

What is no doubt remarkable is that on many counts the United States has a lot more in common with Asian societies than with Europe. Judt enumerates those areas: "in its widespread religiosity and the place of God in its public affairs, its suspicion of dissent, its fear of foreign influence, its unfamiliarity with alien lands, and its reliance upon military strength when dealing with them."[17] America executes prisoners on a scale matched only in China, Iran and Saudi Arabia. Since 2000, there have been more than 230 shootings at American schools and universities. More than 200 students have been killed, and at least 200 more have been injured. In Europe, by contrast, there has not been a major high-casualty gun attack on a campus in a decade. And when it comes to religion, while the United States has a religious make-up broadly similar to that of many European countries, with most people describing themselves as Christian, Americans are much more religious than Western Europeans. Almost two-thirds of Americans attend religious services at least monthly compared to 31 per cent of Western Europeans, including 37 per cent in Ireland who said they do so, 22 per cent in France, and 24 per cent in Germany.

Might we then conclude that Europeans are right and that America deserves to be placed alongside those Asian societies which, for all their progress, remain more or less shackled by tradition? Well, only if we want to confuse everything. The United States has been for more than a hundred years the very image of modernity. In the postwar decades it appealed to European intellectuals such as Sartre on account of its deracinated life. The music, the literature, the architecture of those years were an extravaganza of countercultural passion, breaking with every convention. If we now feel that Americans are after all too conventional, there is reason to suspect that something else is happening and that their love affair with religion, guns and the death penalty is to be explained from sources other than the persistence of traditional structures. I will offer an alternative explanation, looking in turn at these three peculiarities of American culture.

On guns, it is often said that the United States finds it hard to approve gun control laws because its political culture favours self-reliance and what many of the Founding Fathers called a spirit of vigilance against state power. There is something to this, of course, as there is something to the notion that the deep pockets of the National Rifle Association have been and may well continue to be a powerful factor. But the hold of guns on the American psyche is deeper. For vast numbers of people, they express a driving force not capable of being explained by rational causes. In a recent book, Kurt Andersen suggests that firing a gun is to have one's imagination tangled up with fantasies of power, fantasies which of course have terrible real-world consequences. Gun owners imagine they are militiamen, Wild West cowboys, marines in a war zone, heroes and anti-heroes played by Clint Eastwood, Rambo or Neo. Specific fantasies now include attacks by jihadi terrorists stopped by armed random civilians, and the uprising scenario where patriots will again be obliged to become rebels, this time to defend liberty against their own government. "Why did gangsters and wannabe gangsters start holding and firing their handguns sideways, parallel to the ground, even though that compromises their aim and control? Because it looks cool, and it began looking cool after filmmakers started directing actors to do it."[18] Just like a movie. And in fact very few movies—outside the romantic comedy genre—could do away with guns.

The argument for the death penalty is inspired by many of the same drives. Every survey of public opinion in America shows that support for the death penalty is overwhelmingly based on ideas of individual responsibility. Linking crime and punishment is one of the simplest, irreducible plot components in human stories, where the two are shown to fit or punishment to follow from the crime in a logical manner. We long for a proper ending, the necessary consequence of what comes before and with nothing else after it, and the death penalty seems to many to provide closure to the worst forms of violence and grief—an argument that has no doubt encouraged emotional manipulation by the media industry. For its supporters, all justice is poetic justice, the idea that works of fiction should inspire proper moral behaviour in their audience by illustrating the triumph of good over evil.

And, finally, religion. There are deep misconceptions between Europeans and Americans on this question. When Europeans are told that Americans are predominantly religious, they assume that the term means the same in Europe and America. In that case, America would indeed be a traditional society, ruled by a fixed moral code and essentially at odds with many of the structures of the modern world. It would be a society founded on a revealed and more or less indisputable set of truths ruling over individual conduct and beliefs.

But we know that this is not how Americans experience religion. To understand that, we first need to realize that there are other reasons one might choose to be religious other than belief in the truth of revelation. Many religious men and women in modern times had no doubts that religion was false, that it could only be false—modern science had taught them that much—but still thought that a religious life was superior to every alternative. Not because it was true but because it was more interesting. The categories of religious experience were conducive to an intensification and deepening of everyday life. They expanded the sphere of our concerns in both time and space, turning us into creatures of the world and of eternity. And they transformed life into a deadly gamble, where salvation could be won or lost in the flick of a moment. As we saw above, this was how William James thought that religion should be understood.

The centre of gravity of religious experience in America shifted once and for all when it became, before all else, a television affair. As Neil Postman argued in his classic *Amusing Ourselves to Death*, "everything that makes religion an historic, profound and sacred human activity is stripped away; there is no ritual, no dogma, no tradition, no theology, and above all, no sense of spiritual transcendence. On these shows, the preacher is tops. God comes out as second banana."[19] On television there are commercials, promos for popular shows, there are all the other shows one flick of the switch away, so that the main message of the screen itself is a continual promise of entertainment. Religion makes life more interesting, and most Americans, I think, turn to it in that spirit, not in search of a final truth.

There is one final element of contemporary American life where differences with an older European sensibility seem clear enough. Judt does not mention it, but it can be explained in much the same way we have addressed the three questions above. What I have in mind is political correctness. The enormous attention to language, the use of the thesaurus for political ends, the endless battles to control grammar—these are not preludes to political battles for power and resources, but the literary drive to shape the stories Americans tell each other. Political correctness stands for the shift whereby social actors become increasingly less concerned with the way they live and more with the way they are portrayed in the narratives about their lives.

The questions Europeans want to address in the domain of reality—with all the grey misery of reality—Americans have shifted to the domain of fiction. It was James Baldwin who argued and almost proved that race is an invention, but this famous American expat in Europe did not mean to suggest that we should abandon it as an invention. What he wanted his countrymen to do was to reinvent it. Americans have been faithful to his call. Always reluctant to let go of the most intense and most difficult questions of life—assuming in all likelihood that they alone make life worth living—they have continued to obsess about race and the stories of conflict, suffering and edification that race can inspire. I do not believe for a moment that Americans want to build a society where race does not exist. They want to write new chapters in the story of race in America. They will be less bloody, less violent and many times they will be new redeeming chapters, but there will be a race question in America for as long as the country and the civilization survive.

And so we see that a distinctive mark cuts across American experience as a whole, becoming more visible in those areas where it breaks away from its European past. We may call it the marker of a new civilization.

The United States is no longer a European nation. In fundamental respects it now looks more similar to countries such as India or Russia or even the Islamic Republic of Iran. After all, its attorney general recently came up with the following exhortation in a speech at Notre Dame: "This is not decay. This is organized destruction. Secularists and their allies have marshaled all the forces of mass communication, popular culture, the entertainment industry, and academia in an unremitting assault on religion and traditional values." More obviously, asking Ukraine to investigate someone for political reasons goes against everything that Washington has been promoting in the developing world for the past few decades: the rule of law and the independence of the judiciary. America is quickly becoming what it always urged other countries not to be. With an important difference: America is becoming a developing country but is doing so ironically.

FIVE

To claim that television is America and America is television would be an exaggeration. Or is it? The new technology came to life just as the United States became the centre of a new global order. It was the first modern technology to be entirely shaped by American culture and American ambition, and to take the American way of life to its fullest development.

In the beginning the new medium was literally the product of American power, a peacetime application of wartime technology used against German submarines and the Japanese navy. Later, the connection would seem less obvious, but only at first. As the mass medium of choice during the decades when the United States conquered the planet, television quickly became synonymous with an American future of material and spiritual progress. How else could one explain the global success of programmes such as *Dallas* and *Dynasty*? They were a window into America, but a window displaying the American dream in all its glory, a transplant of the American life energy. As Neil Postman once put it, "American television programs are in demand not because America is loved but because American television is loved."[1] A peculiar pattern developed. The United States was becoming less and less competitive in many traditional industries, as the ballooning trade deficit showed, but it was the undisputed world leader in the entertainment and culture industries, where its only rival was video and music piracy. It imported reality and exported unreality.

For decades it remained true that people all over the world were more likely to learn about America by watching television than meeting and talking to actual Americans. And this was not Hollywood with its unapologetic appeal to universal themes. Watching American television was not so different from moving to California or Texas or New York and having to learn all the complexities and idiosyncrasies of daily life there. As a teenager, series such as *Family Ties* or *Moonlighting* certainly created this impression for me. As opposed to a movie blockbuster, television series can become a routine presence.

Science fiction writers have even speculated that, were archaeologists to excavate the remains of present-day civilization thousands of years from now, they might have an obvious explanation for our favorite medium: the television as the Great Altar, a "magnificent structure toward which everything was directed" and representing "the essence of religious communication as practiced by the ancient North Americans."[2]

Arguably, the internet, mobile technology, Netflix and binge-watching did not change this basic fact. By liberating content from the physical restraints of the old wartime vacuum tubes, they can only increase its powers and render it, as it were, more spiritual. With shows like *The Sopranos*, *The Wire* and *Breaking Bad*, television has finally surpassed film as the most creative of all popular art forms, again proving that in America the medium was always about much more than mere entertainment.

I see the internet as an expansion of television culture. The classical age of television still preserved the barrier between content and creator. With the internet, everyone is both at the same time. Every time perceptions are shaped, they become the baseline from which new content will be created in the future. It is as if television characters—not real people living in the real world but purely fictional characters—were suddenly in charge of writing the script. How can they know where the real world ends and fantasy begins? Down the rabbit hole and soon the way back to the surface vanishes entirely.

With the internet, we have stepped inside the television screen and television has invaded real life. Walmart is a chunk of reality: consumers and producers jostle for space inside a giant physical market. Amazon is a television show, offering you a specific vision of reality, tuned to your tastes and receptive to your decisions, with the world reconfigured every time you make a purchase or enter a search. On the internet it is never enough to be. You have to act. In real life you can walk around and by that mere fact be visible to others, but "you have to communicate in order to maintain an online presence." The self gives way to the profile. Online, everyone is a television character. Rather than something that emerges from experience, communication becomes the very point of experience and its organizing principle. "This is why everyone tries to look so hot and well-traveled on Instagram; this is why everyone seems so smug and triumphant on Facebook; this is why, on Twitter, making a righteous political statement has come to seem, for many people, like a political good in itself."[3]

In 2009 Twitter began to roll out the retweet button and Facebook switched posts from private by default to public by default. In 2010 Instagram launched. Suddenly, television and life had become indistinguishable. "Everyone was a broadcaster; everyone was broadcast material." Soon plastic surgeons were being asked to match the settings on Instagram filters and people started to redecorate their houses in order to create suitable backgrounds for guests to pose against.[4]

Television is the secret key to the American century, the primary structure of experience, helping us make sense of our lives in the internet age. It becomes a kind of parent language, furnishing the governing terms by which real life can be expressed and grasped. In a John Updike novel, television is defined as the place where the gods talk to us. "Entering an empty room, we turn it on, and a talking face flares into being: better than the burning bush."[5] In Don DeLillo's *White Noise*, it is "like a myth being born right there in your living room, like something we know in a dream-like and preconscious way." "It opens ancient memories of world birth, it welcomes us into the grid, the network of little buzzing nods that make us the picture pattern. The medium practically overflows with sacred formulas if we can remember how to respond innocently and get past our irritation, weariness and disgust."

What is television? The question is not as easy as one might think at first. David Foster Wallace was on to something when he noted that television, long before the internet, taught us to think of ourselves as characters and our lives as stories. Six hours a day of television—such is the wholesome dose Americans consume—cannot but change our deepest perceptions. If we spend all that time watching, pretty soon we start watching ourselves watching. The people on television are there in order to be watched. Should we strive to be different, better, more real and genuine? Of course not.

Television is addictive because of what it promises: dreams, and these dreams involve leaving daily life behind. As Wallace puts it, the white noise of television is a soft whisper that somewhere "life is quicker, denser, more interesting, more lively."[6] A show such as *Lost*—created after Wallace wrote his piece—is nothing but a form of life candy. Naturally, the more we look at the images of a more interesting life on television, the more we will be consumed by the desire for a more interesting life and thus the more necessary television will become. Some have suggested that the hippie love affair with chemically induced altered states—peyote and mescaline and Timothy Leary's new worlds—

was a product of television. When people started feeling that television did not fulfil its initial promise as a launching station for liberating virtual travel everywhere—a very early advertising campaign had promised television viewers they could "be an armchair Columbus"—drugs were seen as a new medium, an alternative communications system, that promised the same dreams.[7] And then the internet arrived.

For Wallace, television has abolished reality. Here perhaps is the definition we seek. The viewer may convince himself that he is spying on all the people he sees on television, but this is an illusion. Forget the screen; the screen is unimportant. There is a second layer of glass behind which technicians and directors organize what is shown to us, and even the situations being enacted are not situations copied from daily life. They are situations invented for television. The characters in the series *Friends* look exactly like a group of actors performing the role of characters in a television series about a group of actors ... Thus the charge that television lacks any connection to the world outside misses the point. To ask creators and producers to keep their sense of reality would be a nice thought if they knew how to tell the difference between fantasy and reality. In fact, they are no better at it than the rest of us. Today it is the real world which copies television, not the other way around, just as physical faces copy Instagram filters.

Take the much-noticed case of *The Simpsons*. Over the years the animated sitcom has shown an eerie ability to predict the future. Many times one of its episodes contained outlandish and unusual events that ended up becoming reality a few years later. Trump as president, which appeared in a *Simpsons* episode twenty years ago. The discovery of the Higgs boson equation. The Siegfried and Roy tiger attack, the Snowden spying scandal, the invention of a baby translator ... The recurrent pattern has provided a field day for conspiracy theorists of all kinds, but the explanation is not difficult to find. The brilliant writers working for the show, the artists and politicians it depicts, the media and even the American public, all invest their energy in looking for interesting and unexpected corners of the possibility space. They are all scriptwriters. It is hardly surprising that they sometimes come upon the same or similar ideas. If the future is a movie or television script, scriptwriters are its prophets.

We are now prepared to understand why it is actually a big deal that America has its first television president. Trump is a reality television star who filled the White House with media personalities and runs the administration like a television series, carefully staging distinct storylines where conflict and crisis are used to power the plot before the announced—fully scripted—resolution. "Donald Trump is going to be the executive producer of a thing called the American government," said Newt Gingrich. Or, in the metaphysical language used by the television critic James Poniewozik, the real Donald Trump is a fusion between man and television, a symbiotic consciousness. "Fusing himself with the culture's most powerful force, he became possessed by it." It happened like this: "He watched TV, and then he courted TV, and then he starred on TV, and then he became TV. He achieved a psychic bond with the creature, and it lowered its head, let him climb on its back, and carried him to the White House."[8]

As Patrick Radden Keefe has pointed out, *The Apprentice* portrayed Trump as a fictional businessman, all the while blurring fact and fiction because Trump really was a businessman. This was a masterstroke for the show, but it also consolidated Trump's image as the most successful person in the universe, which is something different from actually being the most successful person in the universe. Reality as image was the true innovation of reality television, and Trump made the most of it. The old story of television irony: you may think it is all unreal and groundless and even a joke, but once the real world is consumed by the medium, there is nothing left to compare it to and those categories stop making sense. When Trump announced his candidacy in 2015 he did so in the atrium of Trump Tower, and made his entrance by descending a gold-plated escalator. It was the choreography that the show's producer, Mark Burnett, and his team had repeatedly used in *The Apprentice*. A former director of new media for the Trump Organization told a magazine that, whenever President Trump works with camera people, he instructs them, "Shoot me like I am shot on *The Apprentice*."[9]

At times it looks as if Trump simply does not know any better. He owes his elevation to the highest office in the land to reality television and intends to continue exploring its resources from the telepulpit of the White House. Over and over again he has striven to produce a vision of political events "real enough to be compelling but fantastical enough to be entertaining."[10] All the defining traits of television are there: the episode form, the continued interaction between writers and producers on one hand and the public on the other, and the logic of spectacle taking things to an extreme. The great wall, the witch hunt, the atomic button, the "king of China". As for the direct relation to the viewing public—the *New Yorker* critic Emily Nussbaum calls it "a messily intense feedback loop between viewers and creators"[11]—Donald Trump imitates reality television stars with his furious Twitter activity but goes much beyond television by offering what no reality show could dream about: the prospect of changing the course of world history. Democracy may be redefined as the ability to get the show we want. Even those who would never vote for Trump seem thoroughly entertained.

As many remarked at the time, to the extent that Trump could be perceived as a television event, his election was something of a crossing of channels: no longer a news programme providing a window on reality, but a pulp television series. It was an event prepared by the gradual blurring of lines between genres. Long essays were already being written on how Americans increasingly got their news from Jon Stewart or Stephen Colbert. It was hardly surprising that, with the line between show business and news now so porous, the two might in time become indistinguishable. When the novelist Richard North Patterson was asked why he ditched writing novels for political commentary, he responded: "Because Donald Trump rendered fiction redundant. He is our first novelist in chief." Literary agents publicly complain that a large percentage of the pitches they have been receiving from aspiring novelists are about Trump. Novelists are having trouble inventing new worlds because the world around them already feels like fiction. "These authors are not writing the political moment so much as the moment is writing them."[12]

Others complained that reality as such had been abolished, but they had a hard time explaining what that meant. Aleksandar Hemon wrote a piece soon after the November 2016 election arguing that reality had become unimaginable. Did he mean that reality was no longer accessible or that we had left it behind? Not at all. Hemon was simply suggesting that reality had been transformed—and not merely transformed but, as it were, created anew. What could not possibly happen had begun to happen, rapidly and everywhere. He compared it to the onset of civil war in his native Bosnia. "As I biked to a long-arranged breakfast with a friend, the tree leaves on the ground looked different, contaminated."[13]

Comical exaggeration, but that is not the point I want to make. In those days many journalists and commentators described Trump's election as an earthquake shaking their sense of reality to the core. The question is whether it affected the current version of the world or whether it was the very domain of reality that was being undermined. The latter seems to me more perceptive.

On the morning of 9 November, Hemon kept thinking of one Gregor Samsa, who, the story goes, woke up after a night of unsettling dreams transformed into a gigantic insect. Kafka knew that there is no reason to believe that the reality we know and count on as reliable will not suddenly and arbitrarily alter, but he also thought that it did not really matter. Reality would win in the end. Samsa would be expected to go to work, insect or not. As it happens, Barack Obama had insisted, on the evening of Trump's election, that "no matter what happens, the sun will rise tomorrow." Hemon wants none of it. He has read Wittgenstein and remembers how the great philosopher liked to say that it is no more than a hypothesis that the sun will rise tomorrow. Everything is possible. We hold the world together with our faith in a beneficent universe. Blink and everything will be gone.

This is Trump the fascist. There is another school: Trump the postmodernist. The starting point is that Trump and his followers actually show very little interest in reality or the attempt to transform it. As Matthew Yglesias wrote at the time, the experience of finding oneself in Trump's America was better understood through the movies than through history books. Driving back to Washington after a week in Wisconsin reminded him of Charlton Heston waking from his space travel to discover that he was on a planet run by orang-utans. Except instead of orangutans, it was the Republican Party. A number of extraordinary events seem to be happening in quick succession and the normal rules no longer apply, but as Yglesias goes on to note—and this is a critical point—for all the action of the Trump presidency, everything is "basically fine".[14] There is a lot of symbol and story, that is to say, but in reality not so much.

The point helps explain what some have called the paradox at the heart of the Democratic front-runner's campaign in the 2020 primaries. Joe Biden has described the Trump presidency as an existential threat to the American regime while simultaneously arguing that removing Trump from office will make it all go away, like turning the television or the computer off. There is not a lot of difference between the way Hillary Clinton talked about Trump during the 2016 campaign and the way Biden talks about him now, as if his presidency remained hypothetical.[15] Other Democratic candidates see the current president as a symptom of deep undercurrents in American society and politics, and seem to believe that getting rid of Trump is coterminous with a project of social transformation. For Biden there is no need to take things that far: Trump created an alternative reality, so clearly separate from the real world that it can be erased— Biden's favourite term in this context—without as much as touching the latter.

As Yglesias explains it, after the election there were two basic scenarios for a Trump administration. Down one road lay cataclysm, whereas down another road Trump would pleasantly surprise us with his job performance, perhaps following the instructions of experienced advisors and limiting himself to a ceremonial role. Which scenario have we witnessed? Well, none of these two. Something in-between. Trump did not convert to conventional politics, but catastrophe has not come to pass. Indeed, he may even have averted a number of unpredictable escalatory measures against Iran and North Korea favoured by the national security establishment.

Instead, we had a series of manufactured crises seemingly produced for their ability to grip viewers and voters or a combination thereof. In his inaugural speech, Trump evoked a national dystopia: cities awash in carnage; sclerotic schools; shuttered factories; predatory nonwhites; the crooked denizens of swampland Washington.[16] A setting of the scene, from which everything will then follow. In a *New Yorker* interview, Trump supporter Victor Davis Hanson described Trump as the tragic hero of a classic Western—*Shane, High Noon* or *The Magnificent Seven*.[17] At times

Trump himself seems as surprised that he is in charge as the rest of us and as gripped by the narrative possibilities as the television anchors paying him tribute. Trump is not new: what is new is the theme park Trumpland, which may well be replaced by something similar in the future, a Trumpland of the left.

One might think that some crisis would eventually jolt the country back to reality. I suspect this is a very naive belief. The only truth capable of surviving cynical reason—and cynical reason is the foundation of modern society—is the truth that nothing is real, and this is a truth too empty and abstract to appeal to American sensibility. The experience is that of switching through television channels. Tired of the storyline where the mightiest empire on Earth is being exploited by foreign governments? You may realize this is no more than an invention stage-managed by the Trump administration, but what do you replace it with? The story of how Russia was able to determine the outcome of the election and now controls the administration? That is only another invention, perhaps more pleasing to certain viewers, but no more real. Russian dolls all the way down. The paradox is that you can be sure the world around you is an invention, but not by comparing it to the real one.

In a town hall discussion with *New York Times* staff—one not meant to be public but taped and then leaked to a media outlet—executive editor Dean Baquet frankly confessed that coverage of the Trump presidency in the newspaper had been organized around one storyline: "Did Donald Trump have untoward relationships with the Russians, and was there obstruction of justice?" Once that particular narrative started to look exhausted, readers began looking around for something new. And then, as Baquet put it, "the story changed". Around the summer of 2019 it became a story about Trump and white nationalism. A new organizing plot and theme were put in place for the next two years: "I mean, the vision for coverage for the next two years is what I talked about earlier: How do we cover a guy who makes these kinds of remarks?" That is what we will "have to do for the rest of the next two years", Baquet explained, while confessing that the newspaper was still struggling with the task of suddenly shifting from one vision to the next. "When a story looks a certain way for two years", we get used to it. The most spectacular parapraxis is when he calls the Russia investigation "Chapter One" of the "Donald Trump story". Journalism has been replaced by literature.[18]

Before Trump there was *The West Wing*, a television series whose impact on real politics is beyond question. It may not be entirely coincidental that the fictional President Josiah Bartlett so often reminds us of Barack Obama. A few years separate them, meaning that the series was readily available to help Americans interpret the new style of politics when it arrived. Many young Obama staffers, fresh out of college or law school, found in the unusually realistic portrayal of the push and pull inside the White House their initial lessons in how politics works or, at least, how it should work. The show projected an image of government at its best, and this added an extra layer to a familiar equation: if politics attracts those who want the world to be better and more intense than daily life, *The West Wing* was politics transformed. During the years of the Bush presidency it offered a kind of counterfactual narrative of what America and the world might look like had Al Gore won in 2000. As its creator and producer, Aaron Sorkin, unashamedly put it, the series would play a redemptive role for America, restoring confidence in public institutions and pointing a way forward for democratic politics. If the Trump presidency looks like a television show rather than reality, that was true already of the Obama presidency. The difference? Sorkin instead of Mark Burnett. Of course, when those young staffers and politicos finally got their wish to play *West Wing* characters in the real world, they soon found out that the rules were different, that in Washington being the best debater or knowing all the policy evidence does not carry you very far. Was it the real world? Or were they suddenly actors in the wrong political show?

Jeet Heer is correct in saying that Trump is not really about Trump or the product of a fluke election, but a vivid example of the world of contemporary America, where commerce and the media reward performance above truth-telling or, rather, in terms borrowed from Freud, the pleasure principle above the reality principle. It increasingly looks to be the case that the only way to fight Trump is to borrow some of his postmodern tactics or sensibility, putting them in the service of different political ends.[19] Where Heer goes astray is when he claims that Trump's appeal is based on his promise to return to an earlier, simpler era, making him vulnerable to the appeal of the past, when truth and reality were still in charge. He underestimates the irony, the knowingness, the sophistication of Trumpland. Nothing about the new America can be called old.

The year *The Apprentice* ended, Trump made one of his final moves towards the presidency. "It's the hostile takeover of Donald Trump!" announcers screamed, as Trump pounded his billionaire friend Vince McMahon, the man behind World Wrestling Entertainment (formerly the World Wrestling Federation). In an odd foretaste of things to come, McMahon shouted during the match that 95 per cent of those wanting Trump to win were idiots and the future president replied, "To me, they look like a very smart group of people." Entering the ring was an appropriate move for Trump because pro wrestling is on the one hand an expression of classical storytelling—with its villains and heroes—and on the other a supreme form of storytelling that no longer aspires to realism. As Kurt Andersen puts it, the rise of pro wrestling marks the moment when Americans became comfortable with fantasy and stopped longing for the real world.[20] And as some have noted, there is a historical echo as well. Commodus, the Roman emperor responsible for initiating the decline of the Roman Empire "from a kingdom of gold to one of iron and rust", shocked his contemporaries by taking to the arena and engaging in actual gladiatorial combat. For an emperor to do such a thing was considered scandalous and disgraceful, but Commodus strongly believed himself to be the reincarnation of Hercules and ordered that people call him "Hercules, son of Zeus". Trump would no doubt point out that, ruthless and amoral as Commodus may have been, it was his life that was turned into a blockbuster movie rather than that of his father, the philosopher Marcus Aurelius. Eric Trump even wrote a column quoting "the great Marcus Aurelius from *The Gladiator*".[21]

In a curious moment in 2019, while sitting next to Nato Secretary General Jens Stoltenberg, Donald Trump spoke briefly about Germany and expressed his great respect for the country—notwithstanding differences on defence commitments—before adding in one of his personalized digressions: "My father was German, born in a very wonderful place in Germany." This was false, of course, but false in a rather strange and perplexing way. Firstly, Trump said it with full conviction, and on such matters conviction should suffice. Secondly, there is no dispute that the claim is false and the truth about it is readily available to everyone on the internet, where even the birth certificate can be inspected: Frederick Christ Trump was born in the Bronx in 1905. Why would someone choose to lie on a matter where he must know he is lying and where there is no doubt he will be caught, triggering a renewed wave of commentary about his ingrained and irremediable mendacity?

A number of explanations were quickly proffered. The most sophisticated is an adaptation of important academic theories of authoritarianism and totalitarianism. Hannah Arendt, for example, wrote eloquently about the way the regimes of Hitler and Stalin relied on the consistent and total substitution of lies for truth in order to confuse the populace and create the conviction that power rather than truth is the final arbiter of obedience.

Many contemporary political commentators were fed on a strict Arendt diet during their college and grad school years, so the theory immediately appealed to them. Trump must be taking a leaf from totalitarian regimes in the past. By debasing the currency of truth he hopes to create the foundations for a deeper attack on the democratic regime in the future. The former *New York Times* book editor Michiko Kakutani writes that Trump is the apotheosis of all the broader, intertwined attitudes undermining truth today, from the merging of news and politics with entertainment, to toxic polarization, to the growing populist contempt for expertise.[22] Masha Gessen has compared Trump to Putin on the grounds that they lie in the same way and for the same purpose: "to assert power over truth itself." In March 2014 Putin claimed that there were no Russian troops in newly annexed Crimea; a month later he affirmed that Russians troops had been on the ground. Throughout 2014 and 2015, he repeatedly denied that Russian troops were fighting in eastern Ukraine; in 2016 he easily acknowledged that they were there. The point is not to deceive, because the truth is readily available. Rather, Putin lies in order to show he can get away with it. "The king of reality."[23] Gessen does not think Trump is much different.

Another explanation I have heard is that Trump is behaving like a mafia boss. Untruth as a display of power: only the powerful can get away with lying, and making their subordinates repeat their falsehoods is an effective way to test their loyalty and reaffirm power over them. The explanation is an ingenious one because it makes sense of why the lies have to be so obviously untrue. The ritual of subjection is all the purer if the subordinate is forced to repeat something he and everyone around him knows to be false. Having taken that step, they no longer have anything to lose and may be trusted to defend their leader on less outrageous but perhaps more consequential matters.

It seems to me that the truth—allow me to speak of the truth one last time—is less complicated. In his bestseller *The Art of the Deal* Trump seems to be well aware that his father was born in the United States. Back then he chose New Jersey as the place of birth. Bronx or New Jersey? There may perhaps not be a world of difference, but what seems clear is that Trump, as he puts it on the very same page, wanted "something grander, more glamorous, and more exciting" for himself than what his father had achieved. Is it surprising that, as he moved from the New York tabloids to the front pages of every global newspaper, the Bronx would be replaced by "a very wonderful place" in Bavaria? And it makes for much-higher drama: the European who turns against Europe. Later in the book Trump calls it "truthful hyperbole, an innocent form of exaggeration and a very effective form of promotion." He even explains why it is not a problem if the hyperbole is obvious and public. "People want to believe that something is the biggest and the greatest and the most spectacular." Lying to improve reality is not really lying.

Or perhaps the true connoisseur of reality television is not one to be deceived by the show. The pleasure of watching comes from being able to detect the artifice and the editing while thinking that many others are not as savvy.

* * *

In retrospect, we always knew Donald Trump would be impeached. It is not so much that some of his opponents announced it as a goal the day after he was elected, although their irreconcilability with defeat certainly played a role. Above all, there was a logic to a presidency built on high drama that inevitably led to a final confrontation where the players bet everything on the flip of a card. Could the biggest presidency in history—and the highest rated—dispense with a cracking season finale? Hardly.

Character is destiny. Trump was not just destined to be impeached but also to face the specific accusations that triggered his impeachment enquiry. In the American liberal tradition, the office of the president is placed under strict constitutional limits created in order to constrain power and ambition. Once entertainment takes over, once politics becomes genre, all this is bound to change. If the purpose is to develop the kind of conflicts and drama that keep an audience hooked, limiting what each contestant can do is the last thing you want. Normalcy, regularity and procedure become hindrances to success. Contestants in a reality show are always told to be themselves, which means, the most extreme version possible of themselves. This is what Trump set out to be.

Remember the boardroom in *The Apprentice*, the place where everything is finally decided. There are no rules in the boardroom—nothing matters beyond surviving. Contestants are encouraged to undermine and betray their colleagues, flatter their boss, and as Trump puts it in one episode, be overly aggressive. And why not? It keeps the audience enthralled and the audience—having an audience—comes before everything else. "There is no being happy for your teammates. The success of another is a wound to be nursed and avenged." As James Poniewozik writes, "the boardroom would be a direct blueprint for Trump's administration, a dogpile of competitors, cronies, and relatives throttling one another daily for survival."[24] The former White House Chief of Staff Reince Priebus once described the chaos in florid language: "When you put a snake and a rat and a falcon and a rabbit and a shark and a seal in a zoo without walls, things start getting nasty and bloody."

As it turned out, *The Apprentice* was a blueprint for the administration in the more general sense that Trump looked at the contest against his Democratic opponents as a game with few or no rules. Those who follow the rules—what they believe to be the rules—are destined to lose.

It is easy to see what Trump was thinking in the weeks leading up to his infamous call with Ukrainian President Volodymyr Zelensky. In the polls, Joe Biden looked certain to become his main opponent in the race for reelection, but Biden had a chink in his armour. His son had been involved with a number of shady businessmen in Ukraine, while Biden himself was in charge of Ukraine policy in the Obama administration. If these connections were exposed, the former vice president would struggle to shake off the shadow of illicit activities, much like Hillary Clinton struggled to clear herself from doubts over her use of a private server to receive classified emails.

As it happened, the United States had all the leverage to force Ukraine to open an investigation into the Bidens. When Trump sat down for his conversation with Zelensky in July 2019, he knew the Ukrainian president was desperate to be reassured that the United States would continue the military assistance program to his country. In the hushed tones of a mafia boss, Trump never openly suggested a quid pro quo, but in a sentence bound to be quoted in future history books, he turned from the matter of American assistance to Ukraine to the investigations he wanted opened by saying: "I would like you to do us a favor, though." It made me remember the Clinton impeachment, where everything hinged on the meaning of the word "is". Clinton argued that "there is nothing going on between us" because he had no ongoing relationship with Lewinsky at the precise time he was questioned. This time everything hinged on the meaning of the word "though".

The subsequent hearings in the House of Representatives revealed what everyone already suspected: the substance of the investigations was immaterial. What Trump wanted was for them

FIVE

to be announced in a television interview. As the Ambassador to the European Union Gordon Sondland—a major character in the plot—would put it in his House hearing, the Ukrainian president "had to announce the investigations. He didn't actually have to do them." Having entered the media bloodstream, the news would slowly work its poison.

There is no doubt that Trump felt compelled to take advantage of the opportunity, even if it meant using the defence budget to advance his political interests or interfering with a judicial process—forms of corruption the United States would normally be lecturing Ukraine to eliminate. It is not difficult to imagine those around Trump—particularly Rudy Giuliani—pushing the president to go ahead and pull the trigger, perhaps adding that Joe Biden would do the same in his place. Interestingly, the whole affair is likely to have begun as a serious of conspiracy theories accusing Clinton and Biden of organizing their own secret plots in Ukraine. Fantasy politics from beginning to end.

Be that as it may, Trump did make the compromising proposal in the July phone call and the meetings in Kyiv and elsewhere organized by his representatives were even clearer on purpose and method.

As the impeachment inquiry was launched it quickly became obvious that, while Democrats were working under the assumption that Trump's actions typified a serious violation of constitutional rules, Republicans agreed with the president. There was no chance they would vote to convict him in the Senate trial at the end of the process. Politics is a tough business, you could see them arguing: Trump had used somewhat underhanded means to go after his opponent, but did not the fact that he actually scuppered the blow show that it was all a game, with no serious consequences? Above all, with no consequences for the safety and prosperity of Americans. How could you impeach the president during the longest Wall Street bull market in history? And again: the other side was using similar methods.

Predictably, the logic of the reality show did not end when the impeachment enquiry was launched. This time, as opposed to Watergate, no one was interested in finding out the truth. The question of how much the president knew and when did he know it was replaced with the question of how serious he was and how serious should everyone else be.

As the journalist David Rothkopf noted on Twitter, the general feel of the moment seemed more like some great game than it did a battle to restore a damaged nation. During Watergate, the major actors had gravitas. They knew the stakes and they realized that history was the audience that would ultimately judge them. If Watergate happened on television—already a momentous change in itself—the Trump impeachment *was* television. As much as Nancy Pelosi and Adam Schiff exerted themselves, they could not break the unreality spell. The impeachment became just the latest turn in a series of plots and conspiracies reminiscent of the hit show *House of Cards*. Removing the president promised a return to the American constitutional tradition—but there was no return.

A piece authored by Jonathan Allen claimed that the hearing of civil servants George Kent and Bill Taylor "lacked the pizazz necessary to capture public attention," exactly how Trump himself would choose to describe it.[25] "They call it impeachment light," he said. Republican Congressman Devin Nunes added, directly addressing witnesses Kent and Taylor: "It seems you agreed, wittingly or unwittingly, to participate in a drama. But the main performance, the Russia hoax, has ended, and you've been cast in the low-rent, Ukrainian sequel." The president intended the Ukraine affair to be a television show and it did become one, albeit with a markedly different script. At the end, everyone moved on.

* * *

Something similar has been happening to the American left. Old rules are being broken and the range of ideas tolerated in public discourse—the famous Overton window—continues to expand. Suddenly, being a socialist no longer places you outside the boundaries of what is politically acceptable. One wonders if it was socialism or America that changed. In a way it was both. After religious fundamentalism, nationalism and free market radicalism gained a foothold on the right, it is hardly surprising that the American left would also start to test its outer boundaries. On both right and left, however, the new currents should not be taken literally, much less historically.

It would always be difficult for socialism to survive as a historical experience when conservative channels such as Fox News turned it into a fantastical bogeyman, present everywhere and in everything. The associations with concrete practices such as statism in Western Europe or the Soviet experiment disappeared. Socialism was now what each individual television anchor or radio jockey decided it could or should be. But then, perhaps unsurprisingly, when socialism lost all connection to reality, it started to appear more interesting and exciting. We apply here, as almost everywhere in this book, the test of reverse verisimilitude: would it work in a movie or novel?

The answer is determinedly and enthusiastically yes. With its unorthodox programme, historical millenarianism and sharp oppositions, socialism was always able to tell a gripping story. It had viewer appeal, as Bernie Sanders was able to show. Running against Hillary Clinton in 2015 and 2016, he presented a much more attractive, a cooler alternative to the staid centrism ruling over the Democratic Party. At the beginning of the speech kicking off his campaign in 2015 came the spectacular announcement: "Today, with your support and the support of millions of people throughout this country, we begin a political revolution to transform our country economically, politically, socially and environmentally."

Young voters flocked to him and many claim he helped them break with the mainstream. It was Sanders who first saw how socialism could be softened and made safe for American voters. His proposals were far from extreme—a public health-care system and a federal minimum wage—and they could be made more rather than less attractive by being draped in the language of socialist revolution. There are two variables at play here: the taste for extreme programmes and language appears combined with a strong distaste for the actual results of such a programme were it to be taken in earnest. Sanders called himself a socialist while running in the Democratic primary rather than as an independent. For Sanders, democratic socialism is "the understanding that all of our people live in security and dignity" and "a government and an economy and a society which works for all." Nothing too specific or demanding. Trump offers Americans the virtual experience of a nationalist regime without its real-world consequences. Sanders could beat him because he is playing the same game, offering the virtual experience of a socialist regime.

The word has become a blank canvas upon which young activists and dreamers can project their personal and political desires. In a curious reverberation of the fame mechanism—some people are famous for being famous—it seems that most people now call their ideas socialist because everyone in their circle is calling their own ideas socialist. "At least in Brooklyn, and the spiritual Brooklyns of America, calling yourself a socialist sounds sexier than anything else out there, without necessarily advocating anything too risky."[26] The new socialism may be described as a theme park where the experiment can be explored in safety.

Ten years ago, socialism in the United States was still politically irrelevant, as it had been for most of American history. The Democratic Socialists of America could count no more than 5,000, largely inactive members. But already public polls gave a hint of things to come. A 2010 Gallup poll found that while

53 per cent of Democrats had a favourable view of capitalism, an equal 53 per cent of Democrats had a favourable view of socialism. The following year, Pew found that 49 per cent of all Americans under 30 had a favourable view of socialism, three points higher than the share that has a favourable view of capitalism. By 2018 the share of Democrats with a favourable view of socialism had grown to 57 per cent, while those with a favourable view of capitalism had dwindled to 47 per cent.

The paradox is this: if we go back three or four decades, we can easily find Americans advocating radical social change who nonetheless would balk at the prospect of calling themselves socialist. Today many thousands are rushing every year to join the Democratic Socialists of America—membership has already exceeded 50,000—but their radicalism is of a decidedly bland variety. During the 2016 election, 43 per cent of likely caucus-goers in Iowa, 31 per cent of New Hampshire Democrats on the eve of their primary, even 39 per cent of likely primary voters in South Carolina averred that they were socialists, but South Carolina Democrats seemed to hedge their bets: 68 per cent said they were liberal and 74 per cent said they were progressive.

Then came November 2016, when the Democratic establishment, home to so many brilliant minds, blew an election no one could possibly lose. It became difficult to argue that the people in charge knew what they were doing. As the hosts of the socialist podcast Chapo Trap House argued at the time, "if you cannot win elections anymore, why should we be playing by your playbook?" As Trump started to wreak havoc in Washington, it would become impossible to argue that only limited changes in policy were possible in contemporary America. It was Trump in some way who introduced the American left to history in the grand style. Suddenly a great fight was afoot as America seemed to enter its dark age, the dark night of authoritarianism and fascism. Cultural referents were clumsily being put together—the

great symbols from the European political tradition were reinterpreted as literature—and in the face of historical tragedy an
equally grandiose response seemed necessary. Antifa or "antifas-
cist activity", the stuff of history books on Weimar Germany,
was one response. Millennial socialism was another.

The freshman congresswoman from New York, Alexandria
Ocasio-Cortez, herself a member of the Democratic Socialists of
America, has turned socialism into the sort of bold narrative that
can capture universal or almost-universal attention. Her Green
New Deal is carefully crafted not as a policy plan but as a quest.
Politico called it "the Impossible Dream of Alexandria Ocasio-
Cortez." She knows that the proposals will never be approved,
but that hardly matters because opposition and rejection are part
of the story. The hero sets out to find a most precious object or
person and the journey is hazardous and long. He or she must
pass a series of tests while facing the opposition of malicious
opponents, both human and natural. In some cases failure must
be expected, not only to advance the story and create tension, but
because failure is the ultimate test of will and virtue. Rebuild
every single building in America. End fossil fuels. Ban nuclear
energy. Make air travel unnecessary. Unionize all new jobs.
Replace beef with cellular agriculture technology.

Ocasio-Cortez became a singular phenomenon in American
politics—capable of drawing crowds to her events and filling
endless hours of cable news coverage—not because of her policy
proposals, but because her entry into national politics was
straight out of a fairytale. Only twenty-eight years old at the
time and with no previous political experience, she broke all the
rules of politics by soundly defeating Joe Crowley, the boss of
Queens politics, who was widely tipped to be the next Speaker of
the House. That a man to whom everyone in Democratic New
York politics paid tribute could be defeated by a neophyte—and
one coming from the fringes of the party—was inconceivable.

The story was too good to be true, which meant that it was the best kind of truth and, perhaps more important, it seemed to promise more wondrous events in the future. It was like the early proofs of valour performed by a knight in a chivalric novel. We have once again become rather superstitious about such things.

Like all quests, the Green New Deal is set in a kind of dreamland, which allows its authors to increase the dramatic elements of struggle and conflict, but at the obvious cost of divorcing themselves from social and historical reality. The detailed consideration of technological and economic forces, for example, is ignored. The causal nexus between problem and solution appears fanciful. Since the authors of the Green New Deal have invented the story, they alone know the logic of events. There are perplexing elements in this logic. Why, for example, would one want to rebuild every building in America in order to increase energy efficiency when we are getting all our energy from zero-emission sources anyway? But a dream world follows different rules from those we know from the real one, which only increases its powers of attraction.

After the Green New Deal was publicly announced, a common pattern emerged. Many of the proposals seemed to evoke an apocalyptic clash between humanity and nature with different dystopian scenarios seen as necessary bridges to a post-human reconciliation of opposites. This was history on a grand scale. Politically it seemed savvy. Republicans responded with derision, allowing Ocasio-Cortez to argue that the critical question is whether climate change will be taken seriously and not the specific proposals eventually approved. House Speaker Nancy Pelosi joined them by calling the plan "the green dream or whatever", but in the process managed little more than reinforce the perception that she can no longer speak for the future of the Democratic Party. The congresswoman from New York is well aware of this. It is as if Lenin announced the "dictatorship of the proletariat" not as something to be done but as a catchy title allowing him to control the narrative.

The point is to tell a great story, to put on a show at least equal to the historical moment, but to do so from the stable standpoint of society in its current form. The Green New Deal says nothing about how its goals would change the point of departure or undermine the very resources on which it draws. Which is to say: it all takes place somewhere other than the real world. In a video illustrated by Molly Crabapple, Ocasio-Cortez set out to "tell the story of what has not happened yet", as Naomi Klein put it. As a policy plan it seems lacking, but it has everything one might expect from a movie script. The individual flashback, the race against the clock to avert catastrophe, and even that Hollywood classic: how divisions are overcome by means of a common endeavour. There is a hero or a heroine—an imprudent note for a politician to strike—who forges ahead when everyone around her complains that it will not work or the time to act has already passed. By the end, Ocasio-Cortez sits in a bullet train speeding from Washington to New York—is this the extent of her technological imagination?—and reminisces about the past, while a new prodigy girl takes her place in Congress, the fictional Eliana, one of the "early children of the Green New Deal". The credits scroll. The End.

In an interview for the podcast Pod Save America in August 2019, Ocasio-Cortez explained the foundations of her political philosophy: "We have to become master storytellers. Everyone in public service needs to be a master storyteller. My advice is to make arguments with your five senses and not five facts. Use facts as supporting evidence, but we need to show we are having the same human experience. You have to tell the story of me, us, and now. The America we had even under Obama is gone. That is the nature of time. We have to tell the story of the crossroads."

Millennial socialism sees history as a struggle to control the memes of production.

SIX

Two decades ago, when I arrived at Harvard to study political philosophy, the discipline had become a dull affair. Imagine joining a field of study or activity after it has completed all its stated goals. Not Shakespeare, not even a commentator on his plays— you are a commentator on his commentators. Nothing left to do, but the show must go on because there is no one in charge of pulling the plug.

It would have been bad enough if the main problems of political philosophy had already been solved. In fact it was much worse. Every problem—big or small—had disappeared. There was a procedure in place, a kind of mechanism allowing us to determine what a society should look like before we knew anything about that or any other society. The procedure had been perfected by John Rawls, the greatest political thinker in American history and arguably the greatest political thinker of the twentieth century. Rawls had taught at Harvard most of his life. Austere and humourless, he struck his interlocutors as something of a religious figure: "a Puritan in a tall black hat", as Isaiah Berlin said. His thought towered above us, more as a prohibition than as an interrogation. There was nothing left to do. We knew the truth and were sure it was the truth. Every effort to find a new way could only be interpreted as intellectual obtuseness or, worse, moral turpitude.

While the predicament affected no more than political theorists, all might still be well. But as some of us had started to suspect, this was a more general condition. The problem was that liberalism had been so extraordinarily effective at specifying the conditions of a free society that it could produce an answer to every political question. It could produce that answer *by itself*, with no need to revert to the actual people living in a liberal society. Gender relations, the workplace, abortion, religion, technology, money: liberal theory could tell you how to think about each of these and many other difficult questions. You almost forgot the whole point of a free society was to let people decide important questions in their own lives. Unfortunately but unavoidably, it turned out that, by the point an individual was ready to start living, every important question would already have been decided. Not on substantive grounds but as part of a detailed specification of what needed to be the case if people were to be free to decide how they wanted to live. The paradox could drive you mad.

A story by the architect Adolf Loos seems to me to illustrate the point.[1] It tells how a wealthy and happy Viennese businessman, tired of being no more than a practical man, decided one day that his life needed the exaltation and permanence of art. Or at any rate—for whatever reason—it needed art. He called on a renowned interior architect, who duly proceeded to throw out all his furniture and organize a small army of painters, sculptors, masons and carpenters to create a living museum. When the rich man saw his new house, he was overjoyed. There was art everywhere he looked, art in everything and anything. When he turned a door handle, he grabbed hold of art and his feet sank in art when he walked across the carpet. Every room was a complete masterpiece. And then the nightmare started.

Because the architect had forgotten nothing, the house was perfect. The architect had thought of everything in advance and decided everything in advance. You picked up an object and the order of the ensemble was immediately disturbed. An endless searching and guessing for the right place to return it would begin. Better not to pick anything up. The rich man started to spend as little time as possible at his house, which had become a historical monument rather than a home. When his birthday arrived, his wife and children gave him many presents. A disastrous mistake, as it turned out. The architect wanted nothing of it and he was the one in charge. "How dare you receive presents? I took care of everything. You need nothing more. You are complete." When the rich man suggested that, as a rich man, he should at least be allowed to buy new things, the answer came swiftly. No idea could be more shocking. Nothing could be allowed that had not been designed by the architect. Then the rich man, the happy man, suddenly felt deeply unhappy. "He was shut out of future life and its strivings, its developments, and its desires."

To be sure, there were people at Harvard who felt uncomfortable in the newly completed liberal house. My teacher Michael Sandel made repeated efforts to break free. He felt that liberalism was too cold a philosophy, and strove to provide a richer content for human attachments and emotions. That content was to come from community life, but Sandel never risked much in this pursuit. His plan was to enrich liberalism from the inside without abandoning the formal framework of rights and liberties inherited from the liberal tradition. That placed him in the awkward position of having to slowly withdraw the promises he himself had made for his approach. He would argue, for example, that banning pornography was acceptable, but it quickly turned out that he meant this to apply, very restrictively, to the public display of pornographic materials in bookshops and even then only in select communities rather than the larger society. Another time, he told students that a street musician had the right to be paid for his troubles, even if he had not contracted anything with the passersby. There were other grounds for legal obligation besides contract. Students were flabbergasted and Sandel dropped the idea.

Other political theorists at Harvard attempted different versions of the same strategy, which consisted in little more than applying the principle of toleration to liberal ideas, thus creating some space where their imperial reach could somehow be limited. Some wanted a "liberalism of virtue". An assistant professor had written a book advocating a "liberalism of honor". Others spoke of a "liberalism of passion" and, unable to resist, I wrote my dissertation on a "liberalism of adventure"—the strivings, the developments, the desires of life. It was a futile effort because, as I noted above, contemporary liberalism had an answer to everything. To deny that this was the case was to move beyond the liberal creed, and that no one was ready to do.

John Rawls provided a good example of someone who had been struggling with the question. He wrote two major works. The first, *A Theory of Justice*, was a work of mainstream liberal thought, very much in the tradition of such European political philosophers as Locke, Rousseau or John Stuart Mill. In it Rawls argued for a conception of justice based on principles of individual freedom and political equality, while providing some clever new ways to arrive at them. He must have thought that not much could be added and was ready to move on to other issues and perhaps even other areas of philosophy when something happened that could be described as a break—albeit a timid one—with the European tradition.

In his second major book, *Political Liberalism*, Rawls tried to address a serious problem with his earlier approach. How could he have expected the citizens of a modern diverse society to accept the same philosophical doctrine? The American society he had known and admired all his life is characterized by a pluralism of incompatible philosophical doctrines. None of these doctrines is affirmed by citizens generally. Some of them may be so contradictory to the idea of justice that we should feel justified in ruling them out. But many others, surely, must find their place in a diverse society, and therefore the attempt to make everyone think and do the same things is destined to fail.

As we saw in an earlier chapter, all these insights had been developed by William James, so they were not exactly new, but Rawls suggested a creative solution. Rather than affirming a single philosophical doctrine of justice, the liberal state should allow many different doctrines to flourish, provided they all agreed on some fundamental political principles. The result would be something like a diagram with multiple overlapping circles. The area of overlap between all the circles is the political conception of justice, but each group, represented by a circle, has its own reasons to support that conception. A religious group may support the principles of freedom and equality because they are dictated by religious doctrine, while artists and intellectuals arrive at them from the point of view of the creative and eccentric individual. The political conception is a module, a constituent part that fits into various philosophical doctrines that endure in the society regulated by it.[2]

The political conception is shared by everyone while the philosophical doctrines are not. Rawls was careful to underline that the political conception could not be called true. It did not aspire to give a theory of how human beings should live, only a stable arrangement allowing them to live with each other and share the same political institutions.

I was never convinced that what Rawls had presented amounted to a solution to the problem that he and the rest of us were interested in. In a famous passage on abortion, he argued that Catholics may reject the existence of a right to abortion, but they cannot impose their views on others. All they can do is not exercise the right of abortion in their own case. Rawls had reformulated his approach to political truth, but he ended up with exactly the same response to every debated question. Some of the political theorists working on this issue at Harvard would even argue that political liberalism did not change anything whatsoever. Human beings do not have a bicameral mind: what they are supposed to believe in the political sphere will seep into other domains, and the demand for a just politics will invade the whole of our private lives.

I met Rawls only once, during a conference about his work in Santa Clara. Since I had been bothered by this particular reservation about his efforts, I chose to ask him whether he thought a philosophical doctrine could have any reality if its defenders were supposed to apply it only to their own private convictions. In secret you could be anything, in public you had to be a liberal. Was this not the opposite of what happened in traditional societies? In secret you could be a libertine, in public you had to be pious. I later wrote in my doctoral dissertation:

> When Columbus first sailed on that impossible route that took him away from all known land, each day adding a new day to the return journey, he may have done so, as we are led to believe, for no reason other than it could be done. This he had to keep to himself, for in his world one had to act for the sake of the ends represented by crown and church, the service and exaltation of the church no less than the increase and glory of the crown. Consider the situation in which we find ourselves. It would seem to be the exact reverse. We may well want to travel across the ocean for the sake of our soul, or our bank account. These will be private aspirations. We can act only under the assumption that we act for no end at all. The state will issue us a passport without asking what we want it for.

Rawls was not impressed by my way at looking at the question, but I have often thought about that exchange. I wish it had occurred to me back then that the unreality I was referring to might in fact be a great political virtue. Rawls died before reaching the promised land, but he did point to a fundamental problem. Eventually the solution would come not from academic departments but from the real world—or, rather, the unreal world outside.

Examples were all around us, but somehow we were too distracted to see them. They were on television and in the movies and on the internet. On the screen, all human possibilities were allowed and celebrated because none of them were real. Sandel could have argued that the state should allow a community to ban pornographic bookstores not on the grounds that pornography offends its values but because we can all benefit from exploring as many human possibilities as possible. And when his students protested, as inevitably they would, he could calmly explain that all these possibilities are not meant to be real. They are accepted on the condition that they abandon every claim to be true and therefore every claim to override different or conflicting life forms. One could build a traditional community in the spirit of a fantasy park where certain possibilities can be experienced more fully. Think of the television series *Westworld*.

Suppose one were to leave liberalism behind in search of new strivings and new adventures. What then will hold everyone back? What limits to those new adventures would we be able to establish? On what basis could a stable society be maintained? If everyone leads his or her life as if it were a movie or a television series, what stops us from ending up in anarchy or a war of all against all?

When commentators complain that American society and politics no longer seem real, they miss the promise of unreality. The real world has many disadvantages. What happens in reality has final consequences. Many of those consequences cannot be undone. And the real world is one: there is no place there for contradictions or even for multiple versions of the same experience.

Liberal society is based on a principle of freedom: the only freedom which deserves the name is that of pursuing our own good in our own way so long as we do not attempt to deprive others of theirs or impede their efforts to obtain it. Or, as Rawls puts it, each person has a claim to a fully adequate scheme of equal basic rights and liberties, which scheme is compatible with the same scheme for all. The new America is founded on a different principle. I call it the principle of unreality: everyone can pursue his or her own happiness so long as they refrain from imposing it on others as something real—as something valid for all.

One way to think about the principle is to note that a society may be richer in human possibilities if it allows for the existence of illiberal ways of life, but in that case it is the value of diversity or experimentation that is being pursued, not the values defended by those ways of life. Citizens must be at liberty to adopt and abandon different values, to enter or exit different experiments in living. The state must recognize and enforce this right to enter and leave. These are experiments, adventures, storylines. They are not real life. They can be switched on and off.

One could argue that the right to exit is the only fundamental human right. A society may countenance the existence of deeply illiberal practices and groups, provided it ensures every individual has the right to exit these practices and groups as soon as he or she no longer wants to participate in them. The fundamental right is a safe word or a kill switch allowing us to stop the game or experience. Like malware authors, we need to include a kill switch in case we lose control over our own creations—in case things get too real. Provided this switch is available, the game itself may well be dangerous or offensive.

It is important to stress this last point. The experience must be immersive. Doubt and scepticism have a role in human society, but they cannot be present everywhere. At some point we must be allowed to experiment with different possibilities without being reminded of their flaws or incompleteness, and those committed to a certain life form must have the power and autonomy to craft a world that is exciting and rewarding. Intrusions and distractions from the theme should be minimized. Losing oneself, breaking through the screen or the mirror: the metaphors imply a transition to a new world endowed with the richness and consistency of reality. It is what Disneyland already announced: motion picture stories reconstructed in physical space.

The liberty the state must defend is the liberty not to be trapped within ways of life. The state must safeguard the ability of individuals to experiment with and move between different ways of life, but none of these ways of life could be experienced very deeply if individuals were to act as mere voyeurs, looking at the possibilities open to them, without actually taking a leap and fully embracing what is offered. No one will be able to experience the full force of religious belief by being reminded at every step to exercise critical thinking and question the basis of those beliefs. Public principles, institutions, and practices create imaginary worlds for the enactment of individual and group experiences, constrained only by the refusal to use state coercion to impose one specific way of life.

Consider the series *Westworld* one more time. Guests to the fantasy park pay a prohibitively high fee to visit an alternative world, full of danger and excitement, "more real than reality itself", but this is a world where the right to exit or to leave is strictly protected. There are plenty of safety measures in place. The visitors cannot be killed by the robotic androids they meet in the park. Guns are somehow able to distinguish between humans and androids, so bullets simply bounce off them. The park has one basic rule: humans cannot get hurt. The adventures do get unruly and wild, especially as you leave the main village, Sweetwater. There is no censorship on content, no matter how immoral. The whole point is to be immoral. But no one gets hurt, everyone is able to leave, so they can return and experience new adventures in the future.

The television series is based on the 1973 movie of the same name, written and directed by Michael Crichton. There is a lot in the movie that prefigures the development of American society and culture over the past few decades. Visitors leave their boring office and family lives in search of deeper experiences. The theme parks they can choose from are celebrations of value pluralism. Much of the point is to experience new worlds where mainstream liberal values are unknown. The experience is fully immersive, everything feels real, but as much as each guest will be transformed by their time there, they know this is not reality: bullets cannot kill them. The principle of unreality is an answer—a specifically American answer—to the shallowness of life in a modern liberal society.

In a 1972 court case, Old Order Amish parents objected to a Wisconsin state law that mandated the schooling of all children under the age of sixteen. They claimed a right to exempt their children from schooling after eighth grade, arguing that the mandatory schooling requirement would violate their religious freedom and destroy their way of life. The Supreme Court ruled in favour of the parents, a decision quickly criticized on two main grounds. Firstly, many of the initial reactions showed concern that by allowing different groups to live in a separate world from the larger society, we endanger social and political stability, which requires a shared culture and a sense of common purpose. The second set of criticisms points out that there is a third party to the case besides the Amish parents and the state: Amish children have the right to decide how they want to live their own lives, and this right is dependent on developing the skills and knowledge that allow them to know about alternatives and be successful outside their community. Both are classical liberal arguments.

I believe the case was correctly decided. I do not entirely disagree with the two arguments mentioned above, and they must play a role as we fine-tune a solution to every particular case, but the main danger for me lies elsewhere. I worry that an overbearing concern with fostering a sceptical attitude towards existing ways of life has already produced a detached attitude preventing many people from directly engaging with life. We risk creating individuals whose contact with lived experience is at best shallow and at worst nonexistent. The contemporary European culture of café life and momentary sensation is a greater risk than the dangers of *Westworld*. I believe the quest for total immersion is the holy grail of modern politics. A society of stories would be able to create new experiences and genuine feelings and thoughts in a completely artificial environment. The possibilities are endless.

What can hardly be denied is that, independently of its merits, a "society of stories" is the best way to think about contemporary America. For Europeans the two liberal arguments above are intuitively powerful and compelling. Most Americans are unconvinced. What contemporary America exhibits is a world of worlds where the high-tech utopia of San Francisco exists side by side with those parts of the country where many more people believe in heaven, hell and angels than in the theory of evolution. The European will say: there is no truth; the American: there is no truth, so everything is true. The difference between Europeans and Americans is that the former see the great narratives of nation, religion or money as fictions to be abandoned while the latter embrace them all the more for being fictions.

It may well be that in Europe or elsewhere the liberal state has come under attack from radical doctrines advocating a return to tradition, the nation, religion or other substantive values. In America the liberal state is being attacked from a different quarter. American populism promises a government uninterested in the question of truth. Public authorities no longer affirm a set of political truths. They are in the fantasy business. If the state has no claim to truth, every way of life can be freely promoted or broadcast. Welcome to the television society, a place of opposites and contradictions where something completely different is always available on a different channel. As a mass medium produced by many people and organizations and aimed at the broadest and most heterogeneous set of audiences, television is a model society, kept together by its own unreality.

The promise of television is like the promise of America herself: the promise of choice. Not an abstract form of choice like that propounded by European philosophers, but real choice, which is less a mental faculty than a range of readily available alternatives. Everything we might ever want or need is somewhere on television right as we speak. The combinations and juxtapositions are wondrous. Death metal, dedicated pornography channels, televangelists and housewives. And in the news such a range of views as one could never find among parties and politicians. Back in America after his captivity in Lebanon, one of the hostages taken by the terrorists who hijacked TWA Flight 847 in June 1985 mused: "When you go to Beirut, you live war, you hear it, you smell it and it is real. It made me appreciate our freedom, the things we take for granted. When we sit here in our living room, with the sun setting, the baby sleeping, we can watch television, change channels. We have choices."[3]

Stop for a moment to appreciate the genuinely revolutionary nature of the transformation. American populism would seem to take to its logical conclusion the idea that a political conception is no longer true or false. It is in fundamental agreement with the liberal tradition on the question of truth, but draws fundamentally different conclusions from the fact of relativism. Rather than sticking to neutral procedures and promoting a framework of institutions devoid of substantive content, it is in love with the idea of designing and building imaginary worlds:

highly structured simulations that are just as complex and rich as the real world. Democracy is less the incorporation of input from voters than the constant appeal to viewers with new content, new projects and new possibilities. Even if one movement or concept is often dominant, having more access to the public and greater resources, there are other alternatives struggling to survive and new ones being prepared. The goal of the state is similar to that of a scriptwriter: to bring all the different characters and stories together, deciding which should have room to grow and which should play a supporting role or move to the background. Within the democratic process, these choices are constantly open to revision, just as a television series is constantly trying to adapt to viewers. The Democratic presidential candidate Pete Buttigieg said of the Trump presidency: "We need to change the channel from the show that we have all been watching. And that is my response to this presidency." The same Buttigieg once compared a shift from a centralized politics to greater power at the state and local levels—where people felt they could make a difference—as switching the world of *Veep* for a version of *Parks and Recreation*.[4]

Let us review the possibilities. Firstly, the traditional state: it pursues a conception of the good life it holds to be always and everywhere true. Secondly, the liberal state, which refrains from affirming the truth of any specific way of life. Thirdly, the post-truth state, which combines the other two categories. Like the traditional state, it pursues a specific view of the world or rather a number of specific views, but it does this with no illusions about their truth and without taking them too literally. It is fragmentary and composite, a vast stage where different possibilities may be concurrently staged. What follows from the knowledge that something is an illusion is not that it should be banned or eliminated but that we should be allowed to leave it or exchange it for some rival when it can no longer instruct us, attract us or entertain us. Truth, by contrast, is that which, when you stop believing in it, does not go away.

What has been abandoned is the hard edge of truth: the state no longer attempts to shape the structure of reality, as used to be the case with Marxists, Catholics, fascists, and others. The post-truth state is made up of geological strata: the bottom layers are liberal and sceptical, but close to the top there is a thick layer of engrossing life content. Post-truth is not a bad term. The traditional state was founded on a set of revealed truths. The liberal state affirmed that truth does not exist, but, in what seemed a contradiction, actually took this statement as a new kind of truth. The post-truth state takes things to their logical conclusion. The whole world is a stage.

Social movements and ideas which until recently were excluded from the liberal consensus are rehabilitated and given a new lease of life, albeit deprived of the old truth claims. What is not forbidden is permitted, but suddenly almost everything seems to be permitted. Society expands in both directions. New transgressive ideas take the liberal tradition further, but they are joined by previous and previously overcome traditions, so that society seems to move forwards and backwards at the same time. These are not the old cultural wars where cultural conservatives fought against a tide of liberal ideas held by younger people. The temporal dimension, the narrative of progress, has disappeared. It is more apt to say that the spatial limits of human life and human activity have been steadily expanding and can already be said to constitute a vast territory for experimentation, whose outer boundaries remain uncharted.

The main contradiction in contemporary liberal society is that between a politics that prizes routine and a culture in love with the extraordinary event. The contradiction is so profound that even the daily news is at odds and out of step with our most prized values. Everything capable of arousing our interest has a different origin: the lives of dictators, the threats of technology, war and conflict, economic power and sexual malfeasance. Our politics is liberal and progressive; while our culture comes from a different age—the only doubt is whether it comes from the past or from the future. Our culture thrives on great stories, on action and movement, good and evil, suspense and surprise. Our politics advocates a final resolution to conflict and the establishment of a perfectly just society, from which no further departure can be envisioned. Were culture to prevail, politics would be forced to open new, unexplored space for genuine attempts at rewriting the future.

The contradiction found its classical expression in the conflict between liberalism and religion. Europeans chose liberalism. Americans were more circumspect and looked for a compromise, a way out of the stand-off. I have struggled to say anything positive in this book about Tocqueville, but he was correct in saying that Americans have always tried to combine the spirit of religion and the spirit of freedom. It is clear that it was the question of religion in modern society that moved Rawls all his life, including his dramatic departure from the European liberal tradition. He chose to formulate the fundamental question of political liberalism as follows: "How is it possible for those affirming a religious doctrine that is based on religious authority, for example, the Church or the Bible, also to hold a reasonable political conception that supports a just democratic regime?" The emphasis throughout his mature work on the importance in the lives of the faithful of religious convictions, and the need for a theory of justice to take them seriously, drew on his personal experience of religious faith and "is founded on a vivid sense of the importance of religious faith and an understanding of the difference between genuine and merely conventional religion."[5]

In a personal note on religion written just a few years before his death, Rawls commented that of all the views on religious toleration he had read, few had struck him so much as those expressed by Jean Bodin, the Renaissance jurist and philosopher. The reason is that Bodin's belief in toleration was religious and not only political, and his religious faith remained untainted by scepticism. Bodin was the living proof that modern society—unabashedly secular—can grant everyone the freedom to pursue different goals without diluting the strength and conviction of those goals. It is obvious in passages such as this that Rawls understood much better than his contemporaries how the conflict and tragedy of liberalism express themselves. With liberalism we have created a system that grants people the freedom to pursue endless possibilities, but this is the same system that risks depriving those possibilities of the very substance that makes them worth pursuing.[6]

Religion is in the end but one example of a deeply experienced life form, a complex worldview articulating all aspects of human existence. We should avoid mistaking religious scepticism for the larger problem of liberalism. In some sense the religious question may no longer be a living one, while the larger issue exemplified by religion will remain critical. I choose therefore to look at the larger issue from another angle, different from the religious one but related to it in obvious and less obvious ways: the question concerning technology.

The first thing to note is that technology has become the new holy writ, the inexhaustible source of the stories by which we order our lives. When the future history of our time is written, the main focus will be on the gradual growth of the internet as a planetary mind, the impact of artificial intelligence on human society, and the way genetic engineering will allow us to transform biological nature, extending the human lifespan and enhancing human cognition. Already today the news and entertainment are saturated with the latest developments in the tech economy or different technological utopias and dystopias. As Peter Thiel put it in his Stanford lectures—available online—the internet economy has always been fuelled by great stories: "The Netscape arc was reminiscent of Greek tragedy: a visionary founder, great vision, hubris, and an epic fall." The best kind of business is one where you can tell a compelling story about the future.

Since we can expect every grand narrative to be a direct violation of liberal values, the result is that we are simultaneously at war with technology. Big data has become a curse term and the largest internet platforms increasingly appear to us as crime syndicates in a James Bond movie. Artificial intelligence is blamed for unemployment—even before it is widely used—and discredited as a tool of political authoritarianism. It is a strange dynamic that, while creating objects of repulsion, turns us all the more towards them. A new Rawls might be interested in the question of how to reconcile our political values with the drive for technological change.

Much has been written about the growth of a new tech oligarchy in America. To use the term oligarchy in this context may seem surprising, as the new tech giants do not seem in need of exploiting political connections in order to thrive. But in an obvious way they are reverse oligarchs, who may not need special favours or contracts from political authorities but can use being left alone, especially when it comes to regulation and taxes. And yet these oligarchs are also tech oligarchs. The enormous concentration of wealth and power in their hands is ultimately in the service of big projects. Their critics would not deny this. Facebook, Tesla, SpaceX or Amazon want to change the world as we know it, creating a host of new experiences that until recently were the preserve of science fiction: a privatized global financial system, the colonization of space, advanced artificial intelligence, autonomous cars that can be summoned across the country using a cellphone, swarms of delivery drones, and an interface linking the human brain to the internet through a surgical procedure similar to eye surgery ("We will painlessly laser-drill the holes into the skull, place the threads, plug the hole with the sensor, and then you go home"). Bezos, in addition to leading Amazon, runs a spaceflight company called Blue Origin. Among the ideas Blue Origin has been considering is the settlement of artificial habitats in orbit around the Earth, each of them with a potential population of one million. Some of these manufactured worlds would be large cities, others natural parks, while yet others could be uninhabited and concentrate the most heavily polluting industry. Since the colonies would allow the human population to grow without any earthly constraints, the species would realize its potential as never before: "We can have a trillion humans in the solar system, which means we would have a thousand Mozarts and a thousand Einsteins. This would be an incredible civilization." Bezos does think big.

And thus the question arises: should a modern society use its powers against those from whom the greatest historical transformations can be expected to come? Should it strive to keep things as they are?

That a modern society would want to stop the historical clock may seem counterintuitive, but the paradox dissolves once we realize that historical change looks less attractive for those who believe that we already live in a fundamentally just—in a nearly perfect—society. If our societies exist at the end of history and our values express the final development of human reason, the promise of technology to take us to unimaginable futures acquires nearly criminal hues. The power and resources needed to satisfy the wildest dreams of the tech oligarchy would usher in a society where an increasingly greater share of economic wealth would be generated by a smaller group of highly creative people, while everyone else would increasingly subsist on welfare and random and randomly available gig work. To the monopolization of existing and future industries, the tech oligarchs add the control and manipulation of the main sources of information. Unless checked, they could accumulate the power to create a radically unequal and unfree society, what Antonio García Martínez calls a kind of feudalism with better marketing. As he describes it, the San Francisco economy has already produced four distinct classes or even castes: an inner party of venture capitalists and entrepreneurs, an outer party of skilled professionals, a service class confined to the gig economy, and the Untouchable class of the homeless and addicted—a rigid caste system, "antithetical to both liberal democracy and the American project."[7]

Martínez reserves his praise for the European social model, which he thinks does not confine the poor to a separate world. The problem, of course, is the one to which Rawls alerted us in the case of religion. Liberals want to believe they are fighting the clerical establishment or the tech oligarchy. In fact they are fighting religion and technology. The same people who tell us we are free to do everything we want will quickly add that we should keep very quiet or else the magnificent edifice of freedom might be shaken too hard. They are like the architect in the Loos story. In Europe, liberal society will survive and perhaps even thrive, except when it comes to the freedom to go to new places and explore new possibilities, exactly what liberal society was created for. What liberalism gives, liberalism takes away. That, in brief, is the conundrum.

Peter Thiel once told me that he thought fear of success rather fear of failure explains the current economic and technological malaise in Europe. There is a lot to this. What is fear of success? It is the belief that by being successful one will attract more and more scrutiny, criticism and invasive regulation or state action of different kinds. Freedom is approved as an abstract possibility, but on condition that it should not be used. And thus a European entrepreneur is likely to cash in his big idea quickly so he can spend his or her time travelling around the world, having romantic affairs and meeting interesting people. In Silicon Valley they would be mocked as being in the "lifestyle business".

Interestingly, the idea has a certain correlate in capital markets. As Thiel likes to point out, finance plays a much more important role if the future is indefinite. In a definite future, money is a means to a specific end. In an indefinite future it is pure optionality. In a world where specific purposes can get you in trouble, finance may become the only game in town. It can be really strange. Someone builds a successful company and sells it. Not knowing what to do with the money, he gives it to a bank. The bank does not know what to do with the money and gives it to a portfolio of institutional investors. Investors give it back to the original investor, and so on and so forth.

In the light of the above, consider the following matrix. At one extreme, technology is imposed from above. Society is ruled according to a single, dominant vision of the future and moves in a predetermined direction. Liberal political societies are fragmented and diverse, with social forces moving in different directions, often resulting in a noisy and agitated state of paralysis. But authoritarian societies can move in unison. Opposing forces are co-opted or eliminated for the sake of quick and dramatic results. Technology and success are almost synonymous.

At the other extreme, technology becomes the object of social and political resistance, even widespread suspicion. Tech entrepreneurs are forced to cede control of their core activities to society. In practice this means that the full ambition of their projects is sacrificed. Technology is placed in the service of already existing social relations and structures rather than the transformation of social life in its current form. Regulation will attempt to block the disruptive impact of new technologies, and forms of collective control may be established. A right to privacy forbids the aggregation of personal data, even when fully anonymized. As a result, data may well lose all economic value. As a British writer argues in a recent book, "in the coming few years either tech will destroy democracy and the social order as we know it, or politics will stamp its authority over the digital world."[8]

My claim is that these two extremes approximate the political models being pursued in China and Europe, respectively. The middle path—is a middle path possible?—is represented by Silicon Valley.

Gregory Ferenstein polled dozens of Valley founders and entrepreneurs in order to determine how they think about political and social relations. The results support the view that the tech elite in America has few or no doubts about the value of economic inequality.[9] It believes that technological innovation is highly dependent on skills that very few individuals can possess. From coding to venture capital, the Valley is the land of insight-based labour. "A great lathe operator commands several times the wage of an average lathe operator," Bill Gates once said, "but a great writer of software code is worth 10,000 times the price of an average software writer." A society where innovation plays a larger and larger role is thus one where an increasingly greater share of economic wealth will be generated by a small segment of creative individuals. Mass change starts with one person or a very small group of people. Inequality is a feature, not a bug.

Predictably, the tech elite is highly critical of regulation aimed at limiting or slowing down the impact of new technologies on society. It believes that we must leave creative individuals alone and it hopes that the radical freedom of the internet can be preserved as the digital and physical worlds merge together. But this is not the full picture, as Ferenstein documents. The Valley tech elite is so enamoured of the eureka moment of pure insight that it resists coming back to Earth in order to give a final shape to social relations. Technological possibilities are reveries rather than realities. This is not the Chinese Communist Party, which knows exactly how society should be organized. Better leave that to each individual. The tech elite may dream of a future world but is not necessarily interested in finding a role for everyone else in those dreams.

We should not be too surprised that a growing number of Silicon Valley luminaries, such as Facebook co-founder Chris Hughes or Sam Altman, president of a leading start-up accelerator, have come out in support of a universal basic income. In 2017 Mark Zuckerberg defended the idea in his Harvard commencement speech. Unconditional and universal cash transfers are not a new incarnation of the welfare state. Rather, basic income aims to create a fluid society where a growing number of people can pursue their visions of personal and collective happiness, even if only a tiny number of them can be expected to succeed. Again, the liberty the state must defend is the liberty not to be trapped within ways of life. In code: if trapped, then exit.

But the people released from their chains are not only or not even primarily the recipients of a universal basic income. The reluctance to deal with social reality means that the tech elite in the United States will try to blunt the impact of technology—half of all existing jobs may soon be put at risk by artificial intelligence and automation—by providing each person with a minimum payment, regardless of income or need. The idea is to remove the most divisive social questions from the technological equation. Not only would a universal basic income insulate future workers from poverty, it could also quell social unrest and deflate the demands for regulatory oversight. A universal income could provide the tech elite with the freedom it so desperately needs. It is as if we were trying to create a safe playground where every technological dream can be freely pursued because no one will be seriously damaged or harmed by it. The principle of unreality: everything is possible, but nothing is true.

Will it work? Will the unreality principle work as a new political theory for a new America? I cannot be sure, but returning to our matrix it is easy to see why the new America can feel confident in itself. Europe wants to live at the end of history but feels increasingly powerless to keep history at bay. And China, continuously "seeking truth from facts", will awaken in many a strong desire for less truth and fewer facts.

SEVEN

In the summer of 2002, Karl Rove arranged a meeting with the journalist Ron Suskind in order to tell him that reality—the whole of reality—was a thing of the past. Rove was the most senior and most famous advisor to President Bush, the mastermind behind his election almost two years earlier, and the meeting with Suskind happened at a time when the Iraq War was looming closer and closer. The public debate revolved around all kinds of forensic evidence and intelligence reports, taken more or less seriously by the members of what Rove called the "reality-based community"—people who were emotionally attached to reality, the way their ancestors were attached to God.

Suskind did not disagree. He liked to believe that solutions emerge from the "study of discernible reality", but when he started to mumble something about the values of the Enlightenment and the ideal of empiricism, Rove cut him off. "Not the way the world really works anymore. We are an empire now, and when we act, we create our own reality. And while you are studying that reality, we will act again, creating other new realities, which you can study too, and that is how things will sort themselves out."[1]

It was a brazen statement. Many of us will shudder thinking how the most powerful country on Earth could have been organized around the deliberate denial of objective reality and acted accordingly in its foreign relations, where every issue raises powerful passions and deadly risks, where prudence and moderation have a particular urgency. And yet there was something deeply traditional about the statement as well. Americans have always created their own reality, even if they were not always conscious of the fact or as ready to make it a cornerstone of their political practice as in more recent years. America was invented by makers of worlds, manufacturers of new realities.

Is that the meaning of destiny? One original act so imprinted itself upon the American story that all later developments can be seen as its slow but inevitable realization?

The Puritans and soldiers of fortune who left England for the New World are remembered as heroes braving the ocean and the wilderness—alternatively, saints and founders—but this particular mythology leaves out the many more like them who chose to stay. The colonists faced the dangers of hunger and epidemics, hurricanes and grasshoppers, savage men and wild beasts, and were often on the verge of extinction. Their brethren who stayed behind faced something worse: the political and economic outlook in England. The struggles in the New World lasted but a moment by comparison to the long struggle which was just starting in England for a new society where men and women could worship as they pleased and where economic opportunities extended beyond the great noble houses. On one side of the Atlantic, the hard and risky enterprise to change social reality, to swerve it from its path and take it somewhere else. On the other side, the very different plan to create a new and alternative world. By the beginning of the twentieth century, as H.G. Wells saw it, there was something similar between the Americans he met and the Englishmen from the industrial North. The liberalism of the eighteenth century and the material progress of the nineteenth had made them both, "out of the undifferentiated Stuart Englishman" of the seventeenth. "But the one grew inside a frame of regal, aristocratic, and feudal institutions, and has chafed against it, struggled with it, modified it, strained it, and been modified by it, but has remained within it; the other broke it and escaped to complete self-development."[2] The two master plans would eventually converge, but they could hardly be more different. One was an exercise in political and social engineering, bringing together several generations of intellectuals, educators, politicians and revolutionaries—the Enlightenment. The other was a determined flight from reality, the resplendent image of a dream world—the waking dream, sometimes the nightmare.

I have written in this book about the process by which the original gesture came to be assimilated and embraced, no longer as a single moment but as character and destiny. Babbitt already understood that if America was to escape from both revolutionary turmoil and deadly conformity, only one way remained: the American dream, taken more literally than ever before. The frontier settlers and pioneers had shown the way. When social conditions became too hard, one left to build a new world from scratch. Indeed, the cowboy inhabited a fantasy world well before Disneyland and Hollywood turned him into a myth. Over time, free from the shackles of European rationalism and empiricism, American society became the American dream. It discovered that a whole political philosophy could be built around the flight from reality, and this new political philosophy reflected American life better than its rivals. At that point, the United States would be forced to face the real world only when dealing with societies outside its borders, but even this final fortress was, in time, bound to fall. In this chapter I consider the last stage in the process: how the principle of unreality took over American foreign policy and, with it, the world.

How did we get to the Iraq War? How did we get to the point where the flight from reality is solemnly made into a philosophical and practical principle? Rove mentions the growth of

American power, and that was no doubt a prevailing factor in the process. The powerless must adapt to the conditions and circumstances given by a recalcitrant world, while the powerful can impose their concepts and desires on reality. And, yet, power alone is not enough to explain how and why reality became an illusion. After all, power might be used to change the world, to transform it according to our wishes, rather than to create new worlds. We need a second principle. For someone to lose interest in reality it is first necessary that he has tried to change it without success. He has to give up on reality. Power and powerlessness: the two tempos of American fantasy.

Coming out of the Second World War at the height of its confidence and ambition, the United States was expected to try to reshape the world according to its own ideas. That was indeed what happened, but not in a predictable way or without unintended consequences. The law of world politics is that even a greater unit of power and influence, when spread over a larger surface, brings about fewer results than a more concentrated effort. As the theologian Reinhold Niebuhr put it in his classic book *The Irony of American History*, "our dreams of bringing the whole of human history under the control of the human will are ironically refuted by the fact that no group of idealists can easily move the pattern of history toward the desired goal of peace and justice." Since the eighteenth century, liberal culture has been increasingly impatient with the failure of human power to bring the total pattern of historical development under control. The United States happened to become the undisputed leader of the free world at the time when the goal finally seemed within reach—when the control of the atom seemed to render ludicrous the belief that human beings could not likewise be controlled. America became, as Niebuhr wrote, "the prime bearer of this hope and dream."[3]

The illusions about the possibility of managing the historical destiny from any particular standpoint involve a number of miscalculations. Firstly, the power and the wisdom of the managers tend to be exaggerated. Secondly, the malleability of the world is always assumed, presumably on the grounds that it either lacks a will of its own or that it positively yearns for being put on the right course. Some men are reduced to formless material, others are placed high above them as endowed with the supreme intelligence to manage and manipulate the process. The element of irony lies in the fact that a strong America turned out to be much less the master of its own destiny than was the young republic, "rocking in the cradle of its continental security and serene in its infant innocence." Arguably, the United States found itself, soon after 1945, more entangled and dependent on distant lands than it had been before its own Independence War. Niebuhr once again: "The same strength which has extended our power beyond a continent has also interwoven our destiny with the destiny of many peoples and brought us into a vast web of history in which other wills, running in oblique or contrasting directions to our own, inevitably hinder or contradict what we most fervently desire."[4] History may be deflected, perhaps, but not managed.

Writing in 1952, Niebuhr still felt confident that America had the patience and the shrewdness to "avoid the ultimate error of trying to bring the historical process to what would seem to us to be its ultimate conclusion." But warning signs had become visible. Announcing what came to be known as the Truman Doctrine, President Harry Truman made the sweeping assertion that the United States would henceforth make it its policy "to support free peoples who are resisting subjugation by armed minorities or by outside forces." To this day it is possible to debate the exact meaning of the commitment made in 1947. At first glance, it appears messianic and even hubristic. By taking the side of every democracy anywhere in the world against both external enemies and internal dissension, Truman set the stage for a planetary conflagration whose final conclusion must be the victory of either universal democracy or universal subjugation. He added: "I believe that we must assist free peoples to work out their own destinies in their own way." But the literal meaning of these sentences is of course contradicted by the temperament and vision of the people who crafted the policy: Truman, Marshall, Acheson—these were men of a pragmatic bent. Convinced that they were dealing with a master of tactics—one expert at intimidation and bluster—they probably saw the statement of a universal policy as necessary to convince Stalin that his designs would be met with unwavering force. Had they limited the new doctrine to Greece, might Stalin not feel emboldened to attack elsewhere?

George Kennan was not convinced and tried until the last minute to change the language in these passages. They seemed to him to imply that what the United States had just decided to do in the case of Greece and Turkey "was something we would be prepared to do in the case of any other country." And it seemed highly uncertain to him that the United States would invariably—as the universal framework dictated—find it within its interests or its means to extend assistance to countries facing a communist threat. For Kennan, "the establishment of the existence of such a threat was only the beginning, not the end, of the process of decision."[5] He added one condition directly impugning the tenor of the Truman Doctrine as it had been originally presented: it was unwise to suggest that what the United States was defending in Greece was the democratic quality of the country. Very often over the ensuing years and decades, Washington would find it necessary to give aid to countries and allies which could hardly qualify for it on the basis of their democratic character.

As time went on, the blanket commitment to assist every country threatened by communism would be taken more and more literally. By the time the Vietnam War reached its critical phase, the value attached to such a threat called for a response on a tremendous scale. In March 1965 Kennan was convinced that his earlier and deep reservations had been vindicated, expressing incomprehension "about what our people are doing in Southeast Asia. It seems to me that they have taken leave of their senses."[6] Kennan doubted the United States could hope to order the political realities of distant parts of the world when it so obviously was not being very successful ordering them closer to its shores or even at home. "I deeply doubt", he told the Senate Foreign Relations Committee in 1966, "that we can enter into the affairs of people far away and by our own efforts primarily determine the sorts of political conditions that will prevail." By November 1966, during a dinner at Princeton, Kennan was ready to admit that he "personally could not care less" if a united Vietnam called itself communist. For purposes of negotiation he advocated ignoring internal Vietnamese politics and focusing instead on assuring the country's "international status" and its relations with the major powers.[7]

If Truman meant the doctrine carrying his name to be an expression of Cold War tactics, it quickly took on a rigidly ideological character. In Vietnam, the United States was not engaged in anything resembling an equilibrium policy. How could it be? If the goal was to contain China, no policy could be more destructive and absurd than that of fighting Vietnamese nationalism, which had been for a millennium a barrier to the expansion of Chinese power into Southeast Asia. As Hans Morgenthau argued, "in the measure that we have weakened Vietnam as a national entity through the destruction of its human and material resources, we have created a political, military and social vacuum into which either we must move or the Soviet Union or China will move."[8] In Vietnam, the United States was no longer pursuing a policy of containment in the strict sense. It was fighting to give a final form to universal society, against an enemy sharing the same goal. "Anticommunism degenerated into a religious obsession despite numerous indications that the Communist bloc was no longer monolithic."[9] The assumption that history could be guided increased the stakes of deciding who could muster the power and will to guide it. Vietnam was a quagmire, but most American leaders knew that from the start. They were engaged in the impossible task of moulding political and social reality to an idea. Whether rightly or wrongly, they saw no alternative. Eisenhower argued that once Indochina passed into the hands of the communists, Malaysia, Australia and New Zealand would be under threat and the economic pressure on Japan would bring it too under some sort of communist control. It was an absolute task, a problem whose solution could be found only within a general solution to every other problem.

> To ensure the safety of South Vietnam required the destruction of the North Vietnamese regime, which in turn made war with China and Russia seem a near certainty. On the other hand, to disengage from South Vietnam was certain to mean its conquest by North Vietnam, which in turn was believed to be the trigger to a general Asian collapse, again leading to war with China and Russia.[10]

Practically without limits, the goal seemed nonetheless within reach, at least while the memory of the victories over Germany and Japan was still fresh, feeding the illusion that Vietnam could just as easily be transformed into a Western democracy. As Morgenthau put it, "the successes of our European policies have become the curse of the policies we have been pursuing in Asia."[11]

The countries under the American umbrella were then enjoying peace, prosperity and, in many cases, even democracy. The world seemed endlessly pliant, provided enough force was applied and assuming the goals to be noble. But these were two conditions thought to be inevitably joined to American action. It was in this historical context that the Vietnam crisis took place. In Southeast Asia, as Kissinger wrote, all previous patterns were confounded. "For the first time in America's international experience, the direct, almost causal relationship the nation had always enjoyed between its values and its achievements began to fray as Americans turned to questioning those values and why they should have been applied to so distant a place as Vietnam."[12] No better illustration of the paradoxes of history could be found. By entering into the morass, the United States ensured that France would withdraw. By launching a total war, it ensured that the corrupt and weak South Vietnamese state would never reform. By wanting to take American values to the far corners of the world, it ensured that these values would look less attractive than ever before. By affirming the willingness to face the communist threat everywhere, it ensured that American public opinion no longer wished to send troops anywhere. As Niebuhr had warned his countrymen, no one stands above history and no one can hope to control it.

The crisis—the first crisis of empire—would eventually pass. American leaders accepted that Vietnam had been lost, in large measure because the fact no longer seemed to spell defeat in the race to build the society of the future. By then the Soviet Union had been caught in paradoxes of its own. Victory in Vietnam may even have contributed to its demise by encouraging Soviet planners—drunk with success—to run greater and greater risks in Africa and Afghanistan. As for the United States, it had no choice but to re-evaluate everything. A growing literature tried to draw the lessons from the military defeat, the most painful in American history. Kissinger suspected that every strategic cure would be worse than the disease and wrote, in a private memo to President Ford, that there were no lessons.[13] Kennan recommended "total withdrawal, followed by silence and detachment."[14] Others were less reserved.

Two broad schools of thought slowly emerged. One argued that if the United States were to intervene with military force ever again, it must do so quickly and decisively. The other took a much more negative view of Vietnam and wanted to change the structures and ideas that made the disaster possible in the first place. The quick and massive use of force has obvious appeal in certain situations where the risk of escalation is not present and where the goal is clearly defined and limited in scope. Lebanon in 1958 and the Dominican Republic in 1965 provide examples of limited interventions where overwhelming force was used in order to keep the mission to a minimum. In other cases, with higher risks, decisive military action could have unpredictable consequences.

The second school starts from this consideration to argue that the errors of Vietnam were not matters of military tactics or general psychology but of political strategy. The way to prevent similar errors in the future was to develop a structured bias against intervention in every case where no vital security interest was at stake. As many pointed out, once a doctrine like containment had been put in place, preventing Vietnam became difficult or impossible: successive administrations wanted to be able to use force to prevent the establishment of new communist governments. They were not pushed into Vietnam against their will.

In practice, the two schools were not exclusive, and something of a compromise between them could be conceived. No one quite believed that the problem with Vietnam was that the war had not been vigorous enough. Yes, in future crises the United States should act swiftly and bring all its technological advantages in play, but only if the mission had been adequately defined. In Vietnam it never was. And no redefinition of American interests, no change to the legal or institutional system, could guarantee that the use of American power would never again be necessary. In their Cartesian logic these two extremes were appealing to a European sensibility, but not to the American mind. The former extreme would lead directly to a reformed variety of the old colonialism. If the error of Vietnam was that not enough force had been applied, every illusion about the exceptionalism of American empire would have to be abandoned. On the other hand, if the problem with the war was the very use of American military power, only one way to influence the course of world politics remained: the soft power of the European Union, to which the United States was expected to convert. There were some intimations that this could become an active choice—President Carter called upon his fellow citizens to become energy independent and retreat from the Middle East—but they quickly vanished.

> Carter spoke of limits, of lowered goals as well as thermostats, of accommodation with the Russians and other unpleasant realities. That is not only demoralizing in a country that defines itself in terms of growth; it stirs a subtle panic, a claustrophobia, that has haunted the American consciousness all through this century.

Thus wrote Garry Wills in his book on Reagan. The words are just as accurate as a description of the twenty-first century.[15]

By combining the two approaches, a new generation of American leaders invented a third and distinctive way to exorcise the ghosts of Vietnam. Its essential premise was that the United States should remain a military superpower actively engaged in global affairs, but the scope of military action needed to be redefined. Victory started not on the battlefield, but in the planning room. After Vietnam, the United States should never again be pushed into military conflict by other actors and in circumstances it could not control. Every future conflict had to be carefully selected with one goal in mind: final and unambiguous victory. No other factors—much less vague ideological assumptions or concerns about unfavourable reactions in other countries—should be allowed to intervene. Rather than being pushed into wars that everyone would struggle to win, why not choose wars that the enemy could never win? The best commander is the one who first wins the war and only then goes into battle. Henceforth, every American war would be an exercise in power projection, free of the necessities and compromises of the real world. Michael Mann provocatively suggested that the invasion of Grenada in 1983 was "not qualitatively different from the Olympic Games."[16]

When Reagan set about rebuilding American military power, he simultaneously dissolved the link between military might and social or political reality. Supporting the troops rather than actual service in the military became the standard for civic responsibility. He opposed reviving the draft, so that, as Andrew Bacevich writes, anyone joining the military could be granted the status of "patriot, idealist, and hero", while everyone else was asked never to doubt those terms, which distance made mythical and ideal. The change was even quicker in Hollywood. After a decade of portraying the American military as morally corrupt, a new wave of blockbuster movies embraced a new, idealized picture of heroism and adventure. *Top Gun*, released in 1986, portrays the military as a "technologically sophisticated, intensely competitive, and exotic world" where soldiers are indistinguishable from glamorous movie actors. As Bacevich writes, "as rendered in *Top Gun*, modern war resembled nothing so much as a throwback to the days of knighthood—brief, violent clashes producing unequivocal results and followed immediately by festive ceremonies honoring the victor."[17] In the new mythology of war, which movies such as *Top Gun* helped to propagate, the point was not to change the world but to build a narrative of heroism and triumph. Events in the real world provided the occasion or pretext, but under no circumstances should they be allowed to take control. As Lawrence Freedman writes with reference to the Gulf War in 1991, "it was as if Saddam had been asked to organize his forces in such a way as to offer coalition countries the opportunity to show off their forces to their best advantage." On the eve of Desert Storm there was a widespread presumption that coalition forces would suffer against a large and entrenched Iraqi army. Desert sand would interfere with delicate digital systems. The length of the war would turn Americans against it. Although the lessons from Vietnam were anything but clear, everyone agreed that casualties on a significant scale would have the same consequences as in Southeast Asia less than two decades before. That was the presumption, but the outcome of the war changed everything. Up to 1991, the United States seemed to have lost its grip on the art of warfare; after Desert Storm it appeared unbeatable.[18] The lesson of Vietnam turned out to be: fight on your own terms.

One way to pursue the dream of total control was to develop weapons so precise that they could be used in a limited way, minimizing collateral or unintended consequences. The final stages of the war in Vietnam provided the initial impetus and even the first example of precision weaponry—too late to change the outcome, but a significant early response to the strategic challenge raised by the war. Hundreds upon hundreds of sorties had been flown against the Thanh Hóa Bridge, but it survived every one of them. Worse, perhaps as many as one hundred American planes were shot down during bombing attacks over the bridge. It was finally destroyed in 1972 when laser-guided bombs were used for the first time.[19]

Malcolm Currie, director of Defense Research and Engineering, testified before Congress in 1974 that "a remarkable series of technological developments have brought us to the threshold of what will become a true revolution in conventional warfare."[20] Against the challenges posed by Soviet military power, breakthroughs in electronics, communications and cybernetics could be technological force multipliers, a means of countering Soviet advantages with fewer but better soldiers and weapons. The revolution in military affairs changed the nature of geopolitical competition. Gone were the obscure doctrines defended by Kennan and Kissinger. The future belonged to people like Andrew

Marshall, the secretive head of the Office of Net Assessment at the Pentagon, who came up with the simple and obvious but nonetheless novel idea that the United States could beat the Soviet Union by developing revolutionary new technologies. By the time of the Gulf War, strategists such as John Warden were making the staggering claim that it had become possible to design and wage an air campaign that would completely obviate the need for ground troops.[21]

War was being dematerialized. In just one decade the American military had developed a rapidly growing arsenal of precision weaponry that promised to solve one of the lasting problems of Vietnam. By breaking the doom loop between military force and social reality, technology made possible a new type of war: heroic and sanitized, guided by noble ends and scripted in advance. The French philosopher Jean Baudrillard said of the Gulf War:

> The war, along with the fake and presumptive warriors, generals, experts and television presenters we see speculating about it all through the day, watches itself in a mirror: am I pretty enough, am I operational enough, am I spectacular enough, am I sophisticated enough to make an entry onto the historical stage?[22]

It was the first war to have its own logo, theme music and telegenic overnight stars. It played out in real time before a mass audience, the first instance in history that history was shaped on the spot into a dramatic production. There was the Gulf War and the "War in the Gulf". The former quickly gave way to the latter.[23]

The new worldview was neither isolationist nor universalist. The United States saw itself as acting in the world, but it was no longer interested in changing it. Mastering the course of history was impossible. Vietnam had shown that. Instead of history, one had stories: look around for an opportunity to do something great, to add to your achievements, to write a new chapter in the American story. As Bill Clinton proclaimed, we can then say to the people of the world, whether you live in Africa, or Central Europe, or any other place, if somebody comes after innocent civilians and tries to kill them en masse because of their race, their ethnic background or their religion, and it is within our power to stop it, we will stop it.[24]

The Gulf War was no more than an intimation of things to come. By the time of the Kosovo air campaign, perceptive writers such as Michael Ignatieff could no longer shake off the impression that we had entered a virtual world. If the United States wanted to shape the new world order, other conflict spots beckoned, but Kosovo offered an unmatched opportunity to perform a heroic act while incurring minimal risks. For the citizens of the Nato countries, the war was pure spectacle. "They were mobilized, not as combatants but as spectators. The war was a spectacle: it aroused emotions in the intense but shallow way that sports do." For Serbians, it was a horror movie: violent and destructive, yes, but still unreal. Visiting Belgrade during the bombing, Ignatieff saw how newsagents in the streets were selling a bizarre set of postcards of the city by night: government buildings in flames, gaping glass-free windows, the tracery of anti-aircraft fire against the black sky. "No one would have thought of selling postcards of the ruins of Hamburg or Dresden in 1945."

Ignatieff is very much aware of the dangers of virtual war. If we give free rein to our moral imagination, the result may well be a fairytale rather than a better and more principled world: "We see ourselves as noble warriors and our enemies as despicable tyrants."[25] There were doubts whether these imaginary worlds could be built in such a way that they would not fall apart two days later. Within months of Bill Clinton's proclamation of a new foreign policy, Russia launched a crackdown in Chechnya that was identical to Serbian actions in Kosovo. Russian actions in Chechnya were, if anything, more sustained and on a much larger scale than those of Serbia in Kosovo and resulted in even greater loss of life. No consequences followed: Chechnya was real life and real life raises a different set of problems.[26]

Five years after Kosovo, the United States was again at war in Iraq, where it would face a crisis comparable to Vietnam. As Rove argued, the war was an exercise in the creation of new realities. After September 11 threatened to dislodge the dominant narrative of the United States as the global superpower, a response had to be found that could supersede the terrorist attacks, create an even larger historical event, and reinterpret their meaning on American terms. The struggle for meaning—rather than concerns about weapons of mass destruction or the spread of democracy—explains the decision to go to war.

A recent study has argued that the Iraq War was intended to convey a message of decisiveness and power. Afghanistan was not enough to prove that the United States was, as Donald Rumsfeld argued, "big and strong and not going to be pushed around by these kinds of attacks." Only something more spectacular could ensure that Americans would not be living in the world radical Islam wanted for America, but instead radical Islam would live in the world America wanted. If the United States wanted to change Middle Eastern politics and society, as some have argued, Iran would have provided a much better target. But a war in Iran was unpredictable, while Iraq offered a perfect opportunity to perform a great deed and build a reputation for great deeds.

> Such an interpretation would also beget questions for those that believe in the image of the United States as a liberal hegemon, not prone to the dark and ugly behavior of other great powers. The uncomfortable truth may be, however, that the United States behaved as a vicious, aggressive state bent on establishing exactly such a reputation.[27]

It is easy to be in the middle of events and miss the point that they are their own reason and justification. For a brief moment, everything seemed to work. On 9 April 2003, the statue of Saddam Hussein on Firdos Square in Baghdad was brought down by a group of Iraqi civilians and American marines. Some Iraqis threw flowers at the foreign soldiers. The war was over with lightning speed and none of the announced disasters materialized. It was an extraordinary feat, an illustration that a new reality could be built, one where tyrants were defeated and America was equally feared and admired. That the goal was not to build a democracy in Iraq is shown both by the absence of statements to that effect before the invasion and by the notable fact that no thought was ever given to its aftermath. Paul Wolfowitz, deputy Pentagon chief, assumed there would be little need for stabilization and that any consideration of the world after victory was an inadmissible distraction. "I am reasonably certain that the Iraqis will greet us as liberators," he said, which would "help us to keep stabilization requirements down." As the looting started, Rumsfeld commented: "Stuff happens and it is untidy, and freedom is untidy, and free people are free to make mistakes and commit crimes and do bad things."

The point of the enterprise was to act decisively against an old foe and bring him down. What might happen after that was never considered. The connections linking the invasion to the surrounding context, the parallel plot lines, the vast network of unpredictable consequences the war would inevitably bring about or the new possibilities it would open up—all these elements were ritually ignored. If the invasion and the war were a story, they were never imagined to be more than an adventure tale, composed of the simplest irreducible elements of every human story: the hero sets out to defeat a cruel enemy and returns home covered in glory.

The aftermath of the Iraq War was a second crisis of empire, a crisis from which the United States has yet to recover.

* * *

Imagine you were using a computer simulation of world politics with a single input: the physical map of the world, the familiar shape of a large landmass surrounded by oceans—and in one case a very large desert—with other areas forming a kind of outer world. A sufficiently robust algorithm might be able to obtain a lot of interesting predictions from this single input.

The large landmass at the centre—at the centre because of its size—would be the most likely location for the development of world-historical technological civilizations, the place where they would enjoy both the room to develop autonomous forms and the geographical continuity that forced them to come into contact and compete for power. Eurasian politics is politics on a grand scale.[28] But because the competition for power would drain the competitors and bring about mutual destruction, the algorithm might also conclude that a new centre would eventually develop elsewhere and that it might even grow into the main global superpower. At this point, the superpower outside the Eurasian supercontinent would see in a unified Eurasia the single most important threat to its hegemony.

The algorithm would be right, of course. Since it became a world power around 1900, the United States had one permanent strategic goal: to prevent a single power from controlling the whole of Eurasia. Interestingly, during the first half century the danger came from Europe. American grand strategy came into its own when Secretary of State Hay acted to prevent European powers from annexing China. Brooks Adams, a grandson of John Quincy Adams, warned at the time: "Were the Russians and Germans to coalesce to dominate Northern China, and were the country to be administered by Germans with German funds, a strain of a very serious nature might be put upon America."[29] He feared that Germany, being already dominant over France, would ally itself with Russia in order to occupy China and acquire control over unlimited supplies of raw materials and manpower. It was a plausible scenario.

Later the same America joined forces with the Soviet Union to prevent Nazi Germany from conquering Ukraine, the Caucasus and British India. And since for most of the second half-century the danger was Russia, the United States built up Europe and China as bulwarks against the Soviet Union, which in Berlin and Korea twice threatened to expel its rival from the Eurasian landmass.

Now, in the third half-century the circle closes itself. This time the danger is China. One might have expected Washington to use Europe, Russia and India to balance against China's ambitions, but so far the iron logic of the process has been obscured by American triumphalism, itself a predictable consequence of the victory in the Cold War and the collapse of the Soviet Union, which bred the hope that the whole world might be unified under American leadership.

With the Belt and Road, China has placed the Eurasian question front and centre of every geopolitical discussion. In its essence, the initiative is a plan to extend Chinese influence and power over the whole of Eurasia, gaining access to energy sources from Russia and the Middle East, technology from Europe, and large markets in Europe, India and Southeast Asia. Were the Belt and Road to reach all its goals, the United States would become an island on the shores of Eurasia—potentially still very prosperous and protected from direct interference in its affairs, but peripheral and absent from all global questions. It would become the blockaded party.[30] It is a scenario whose dangers were fully perceived by President Franklin D. Roosevelt when he declared that the dream of the United States as a lone island was in reality "a helpless nightmare, the helpless nightmare of a people without freedom; yes, the nightmare of a people lodged in prison, handcuffed, hungry, and fed through the bars from day to day by the contemptuous, unpitying masters of other continents."[31]

Faced with this nightmare scenario, the United States reacted on a number of fronts. The main one was the still ongoing trade and technology wars, in which Washington has dealt a severe blow against China's most successful global company—running Huawei out of markets and suppliers may well doom the company's ambitious plans—and adopted wide-ranging tariffs against Chinese imports. For a while it seemed that negotiations with China were meant to impose a number of onerous conditions on Chinese economic growth and technological development, preserving American primacy in these critical areas, but many reports paint a different picture. When negotiations failed in 2019, the main difficulty turned out to be Washington's attempt to force Beijing into making fundamental changes to its economic constitution, bringing it closer to a liberal, Western model, and carving these changes into its domestic laws. There are two ways the United States could think about the trade war with China: a way to limit or constrain Chinese economic power—and keeping the new tariffs in place might achieve this—or a way to convert China to a Western economic model. It seems that the Trump administration—but arguably not Trump himself, who regards ideological missions with scorn—chose the latter.

Ultimately, decision-makers in Washington will have to ask themselves how this can be achieved. Does the Cold War model offer a solution? Can one imagine a scenario where the Chinese economy would not only slow down but effectively deindustrialize and enter a protracted technological winter? And would one then expect the country to fragment politically as the Soviet Union did? These are fanciful projections. If the United States is to adopt a strategy of maximum pressure against Beijing, it needs to have maximum clarity about the endgame. Does it expect China to change, perhaps after the collapse of the Communist Party? Surely, more modest experiments in regime change have failed dramatically, suggesting some caution on this matter. If, by contrast, the goal is to decouple from China and create two separate economic spheres in the hope that the Chinese economy will quickly fold when left to its own devices, two questions must first be answered.

The first is about the extent of economic damage that such a strategy would inflict on the world economy. Many of the economic gains from globalization in the last few decades resulted from the creation of intricate global value chains. These gains would largely evaporate if value chains were to fragment into two autonomous spheres. The process might well be highly disordered. It might also be conflictual, as both sides would blame the other for the economic pain being inflicted. Which takes us to a second question: how would this decoupling be conducted?

Communism and capitalism during the Cold War were very much defined against each other. By the mere fact of pursuing their basic political and economic values, the United States and the Soviet Union created exclusionary zones, developed over many decades, and staked their future on the success of their preferred system. Today the situation is altogether different. The United States and China are locked in a competition to shape global politics and the global economy. For one of them to retreat from globalization into a separate sphere would be tantamount to admitting defeat in the world game. It could only be attempted as a national project mobilizing all available resources, imposing prohibitive costs and dramatically changing that society which dreamed of excluding the rival from its affairs. Why would one want to decouple from a rival or competitor in those areas where integration is actually to one's advantage? What sense would decoupling make when integration has developed in one's favour or where it perpetuates one's dominant position? The United States wants to use its leading position in global value chains as leverage, but then decoupling is a losing strategy. Breaking the chain is tantamount to losing the position as well as the leverage.

Instead, let us return to the nightmare scenario and see how it can best be avoided. The unification of the whole of Eurasia under a single power is so far from inevitable that it has in fact never been achieved. Consider the sheer diversity of political models now existing side by side across the supercontinent, the imperial traditions of many of the major powers in Eurasia, and the gradual spread of technology and economic growth to all its corners. These are critical factors suggesting that Eurasian political integration remains unlikely—economic integration is a different matter—and therefore that no weighty reason seems to be present for Washington to renew its plans of a Eurasia whole and free, united according to a liberal, Western model and under American leadership.

The main counterargument can be answered with a creative reconstruction of the classical concept of balance of power. The United States cannot be satisfied with a passive understanding of the concept. Balance of power rarely if ever comes about naturally. If we take the current distribution of power in Eurasia, there is reasonable ground to doubt that the balance will be naturally maintained. By combining economic and military power, China remains unmatched by either the European Union or Russia. The former is an economic superpower but a political and military minnow. The latter is no rival to China on the economic plane. India and Japan remain too inward-looking to be decisive factors in the Eurasian game.

When it comes to Europe, the strategy seems clear. It is one of the areas where the Trump administration has made progress. The United States was of course instrumental in rebuilding the European economy and prompting European nations to build the common institutions placing it on a stable keel. The task now is much more complicated because pushing Europe to become a major global political and military power will involve a dose of brinkmanship. It may well be the case that Europeans will not move further in this direction unless faced with a major crisis. And Americans will have to sacrifice some of their immediate interests: the European Union will not create a common defence and security policy without in the process diminishing the inordinate weight of the American defence industry in Europe.

Russia is a much more delicate question. The country has been moving decisively away from the West, and tensions with the United States are now at the highest level since the end of the Cold War. Any rapprochement would have to come from the Kremlin and that will not be forthcoming, at least while Vladimir Putin is in charge. At the same time, Washington risks bringing about an informal alliance between China and Russia. If the approach is to lump them together as the two major threats to the existing global order, they will act accordingly. Even if naturally inclined to develop as independent powers, China and Russia may well feel that the time for disagreements will have to wait while the task at hand is to overturn American hegemony. How does one square the circle? How can the United States keep its distance from Russia's geopolitical ambitions while simultaneously preventing a Eurasian entente between its two great rivals? Every measure it would adopt to strengthen Russia as an independent pole in Eurasia could be used by the Kremlin against its unwitting benefactor, but that should not be a reason to keep Russia isolated. All the United States needs to do is drive a hard bargain in which each concession to Russia must be exchanged for a concrete offer from Moscow to contain Chinese power. When executing a similar manoeuvre against the Soviet Union, Kissinger went much beyond an abstract gesture of openness towards Maoist China: already in 1975 he was pushing the Chinese to build a joint electronic facility in Xinjiang to spy on Soviet missile bases. Today the goal is to find a place for Russia in the Eurasian balance of power—an independent pole between Europe and Asia—while preserving the ability to keep it in check and, when necessary, force it to respect that balance.

As for India and Japan, the strategic goal should be clear: to allow the two countries to grow more confident and outward-looking, capable of marshalling their abundant resources to play an active global role. And why should the United States fear or regret such an outcome? To keep them inside its chain of command, useful only when acting under American leadership, is, from the point of view of long-term American interests, profoundly self-defeating. Only as fully sovereign and autonomous actors can India and Japan contribute to a lasting balance of power in Eurasia.

Were all these steps to be adopted and a coherent strategy developed, the United States would slowly emerge as a great balancer. Its role would remind one of the role played by Great Britain in nineteenth-century Europe: with one foot in the continent and the other one outside, perpetually balancing every European power against each other, determined to avoid a future where Europe fell under the domination of a single power. Its strategists knew that Great Britain would remain more powerful than each of the European states individually, but inferior to their combined strength.

The United States must become in relation to the Eurasian supercontinent what Great Britain was in relation to Europe, but with two important revisions. Firstly, the new version of Britain's splendid isolation—the ability to influence the Eurasian chessboard while remaining sheltered from its affairs—will not come naturally, or in a fit of absent-mindedness. America will not be able to rely on its insular geography and control of the seas. Borders are more diffuse and technology has eliminated distance to a great extent, so a form of forward deployment has become necessary, if only to pre-empt terrorist threats and face cyberattacks and nuclear-armed rogue states.

Secondly, as already noted, the United States does not have a ready-made world of competing great powers at its disposal.

The trend is to return to such a world—the building blocks are available—but some construction work is still necessary. More than a great balancer, America must become a great creator. China has to be cut down to size and other pieces must be built up if an equilibrium is to be the final product. But is this such a great transformation in its general psychology? The United States already regards the future of the world order as a great narrative whose main plot lines are written in Washington. What I am advocating is to replace the epic with the novel: world history is not written from a single point of view and it does not follow a single line of development. It is open-ended and fragmented. It contains multitudes. Every ending is simultaneously a beginning. Every character and way of life can find its place in the great narrative.

The chief characteristic of the modern novel is the plurality of consciousnesses, with equal rights and each with its own perspective; the organized coexistence and interaction of spiritual diversity, not stages in the life of a unified spirit.[32] The narrator should not pick sides, and that is why he and not the characters is ultimately in control. A great novelist allows the different characters to develop multiple relationships between themselves and does not reserve for himself the ability to judge every event from his perspective. The work is an endless dialogue or conversation, where he plays the role of an organizer. This is no longer a story where the narrator relays events from his own point of view, clumsily interpreting the world and everyone in it as a reflection of his personal wishes. Everyone is endowed with autonomy and power; his role is to bring all characters together and preserve their own individual spheres. Suddenly they must move together in a common world and none can be interpreted in isolation. The narrator has learned not to impose a single truth upon the whole, but neither should any of the characters be allowed to replace him.

A global superpower should play at the level of world politics the role that the state plays in domestic politics: allowing for the coexistence of many different ways of life, while stopping all of them from becoming dominant or endangering the balance. As Assistant Secretary of State for East Asian and Pacific Affairs David Stilwell describes it, countries in the Indo-Pacific region "should remain a diverse constellation of stars, each shining brightly, and none a satellite to any other." This is not the old vision of homogeneous states converging towards a single model. Stilwell makes it clear that the systems or models will remain plural: "A pluralistic Asia is one in which the region's diverse countries can continue to thrive as they wish. They are secure in their sovereign autonomy. They are free to be themselves, as Singapore's Lee Kwan Yew put it. No hegemonic power dominates or coerces them."[33]

The goal is to make the world safe for America without making it look like America. In every great story, the main character eventually leaves home in order to discover new worlds and experience new ways of living. It is the same with nations and peoples. Foreign policy is the constant effort to explore the world, but to do so in safety, and on terms one can accept. The tragedy of American foreign policy is the way it fails to respect the mystery of the distant and the strangeness of the unfamiliar.

What the new America needs is the logical opposite of neoconservatism. "Defend your interests in a world that is essentially alien"—a maxim to replace the neoconservative command to defend universal interests in a world that is essentially like home. It is the clash between the protagonist and an alien and mysterious world that propels the story forward and enlivens it with both intellectual discovery and practical adventure. The protagonist pursues his or her mission against the backdrop of a rich and changing lifeworld—many lifeworlds.

For America, the age of nation-building is over. The age of world-building has begun.

NOTES

PREFACE

1. Bruno Maçães, *The Dawn of Eurasia: On the Trail of the New World Order* (London: 2018), 6–7.
2. Hermann Keyserling, *America Set Free* (New York, 1929).
3. Waldo Frank, *Chart for Rough Water: Our Role in a New World* (New York, 1940), 137.

ONE

1. Angela Miller, *Thomas Cole and Jacksonian America: The Course of Empire as Political Allegory* (Cambridge: 1989), 84.
2. Polybius, *Histories* 38.22.
3. Bruce Ackerman, *The Decline and Fall of the American Republic* (Cambridge: 2010), 186.
4. Ibid., 9–10.
5. Ibid., 187.
6. David Klion, "The American Empire is the Sick Man of the 21st Century", *Foreign Policy*, 2 Apr 2019
7. Jeet Heer, "Are We Witnessing the Fall of the American Empire?", *The New Republic*, 7 Mar 2018.
8. David Remnick, "The Increasing Unfitness of Donald Trump", *The New Yorker*, 5 Jan 2018.
9. Tom Holland, "Decline and Fall: Why America Always Thinks it's Going the Way of Rome", *The Spectator*, 10 Nov 2018.
10. Tyler Cowen, "The Decline and Fall of the American Empire", *Bloomberg*, 30 July 2018.

11. Oswald Spengler, *The Decline of the West* (New York: 1926), I, 22.

12. Ibid., I, 3.

13. Ibid., I, 32.

14. Ibid., I, 34.

15. Letter to Crusius, 24 Nov 1918.

16. Robert Merry, "The United States as the Last Nation of the West", in Sebastian Fink and Robert Rollinger (eds), *Oswald Spenglers Kulturmorphologie. Universal- und kulturhistorische Studien* (Wiesbaden: 2018).

17. D. R. Thorpe, *Supermac: The Life of Harold Macmillan* (London: 2010), 170.

18. James Truslow Adams, *Epic of America* (Boston: 1931), 373.

19. Keyserling, *America Set Free*, 36.

20. Max Lerner, *America as a Civilization* (New York, 1957), 19.

21. Arnold Toynbee, *A Study of History* (Oxon: 1955), 57.

22. Ibid., 39.

23. Ibid., 40.

24. David Hume, "Idea of a Perfect Commonwealth", 1777.

25. Alexander Hamilton, "The Utility of the Union in Respect to Commercial Relations and a Navy", *The Federalist Papers* 11, 23 Nov 1787.

TWO

1. "What the world is really about." Well, what the world is really about is always a theory of what the world is really about.

2. Lerner, *America as a Civilization*, 7.

3. *Selections from the Prison Notebooks of Antonio Gramsci* (London: 1971), 317–18.

4. Leo Damrosch, *Tocqueville's Discovery of America* (New York: 2010), 12.

5. Ibid., 18.

6. Alexis de Tocqueville, *Democracy in America*, Volume One, Part One, Chapter Two.

7. *Adams*, Epic *of America*, 100–1.

8. A. G. Hopkins, *American Empire: A Global History* (Princeton: 2018), 178, 181.

9. Ibid., 164.

10. Walter Russell Mead, *Special Providence* (New York: 2001), 17.

11. Henry Adams, *The Education of Henry Adams* (Oxon: 1999), 287, 277.

12. Frederick Jackson Turner, *The Frontier in American History* (New York: 1921), 4.

13. Adams, *The Education of Henry Adams*, 328.

14. Harold Loeb, *The Way it Was* (New York: 1959).

15. William James, "On Some Mental Effects of the Earthquake", in *Memories and Studies* (London: 1911).

16. William James, *Pragmatism and Other Essays* (New York: 1963), 130.

17. Ibid., 38.

18. Ibid., 112.

19. Ibid., 27.

THREE

1. F. A. McKenzie, *The American Invaders* (London: 1902).

2. *Prison Notebooks*, 303–4.

3. Edgar Mowrer, *This American World* (New York, 1928), 126.

4. Keyserling, *America Set Free*, 80.

5. Mowrer, *This American World*, 128.

6. Walter Lippmann, "The Great Decision", in *Force and Ideas: The Early Writings* (New York: 1970), 82–3.

7. Mary Nolan, *The Transatlantic Century: Europe and America, 1890–2010* (Cambridge: 2012), 72–3.

8. Lucien Romier, *Who Will be Master, Europe or America?* (New York: 1928).

9. Bertrand Russell, *The Prospects of Industrial Civilization* (London: 1996), 65.

10. Kori Schake, *Safe Passage: The Transition from British to American Hegemony* (Cambridge: 2017), 241–3.

11. George Kennan, *American Diplomacy* (Chicago: 1984), 79.

12. Henry Luce, "The American Century", *Diplomatic History*, 23, 2 (spring 1999).

13. Edmund Wilson, *Europe without Baedeker* (London: 1966).

14. "Policy with Respect to American Aid to Western Europe: Views of

the Policy Planning Staff", *Foreign Relations*, 1947 (Washington: 1972), 225.

15. Thomas Mann, *The Coming Victory of Democracy* (New York: 1938), 81–2.

16. Essays by Arthur Schlesinger Jr., Allan Dowling, Leslie Fiedler, Philip Rahv and Jacques Barzun from *Partisan Review*'s 1952 symposium on "Our Country and Our Culture", reprinted as "America and the Intellectuals", *Partisan Review Series*, 4 (1953).

17. John Harper, *American Visions of Europe* (Cambridge: 1993), 79, 114.

18. Walter Russell Mead, *Special Providence*, 10.

19. See Richard Kuisel, *Seducing the French: The Dilemma of Americanization* (Berkeley: 1993), 191.

20. Werner Sombart, *Why Is There No Socialism in the United States?* (Oxon: 2019), 118.

21. Peter Katzenstein, *A World of Regions, Asia and Europe in the American Imperium* (Ithaca: 2015), 56.

22. Richard Holbrooke, "America, a European Power", *Foreign Affairs*, 74, 2 (Mar—Apr 1995), 38–51.

23. Robert Kagan, *Of Paradise and Power: America and Europe in the New World Order* (New York: 2007), 60.

24. Ibid., 33.

25. Ibid., 61.

26. Robert Kagan *The Jungle Grows Back: America and Our Imperiled World* (New York: 2018), 137.

27. Ibid., 143.

28. Niall Ferguson, *Colossus: The Rise and Fall of the American Empire* (London: 2004).

29. Ross Wetzsteon, *Republic of Dreams: The American Bohemia, 1910–1960* (New York: 2007), 368, 511.

30. Tom Wolfe, "The Me Decade and the Third Great Awakening", in *The Purple Decades* (New York: 2018).

FOUR

1. Harold Rosenberg, "The American Action Painters," *Art News*, 51, 8, December 1952.

2. Philip Roth, "Writing American Fiction", *Commentary*, March 1961.

3. Daniel Boorstin, *The Image, A Guide to Pseudo-Events in America* (New York: 2012), 240.

4. Norman Mailer, "Superman Comes to the Supermarket", *Esquire*, 1960

5. Gore Vidal, *History of the National Security State: Includes Vidal on America* (2014).

6. With Trump they drop a whole season in one day.

7. Bhu Srinivasan, *Americana: A 400-Year History of American Capitalism* (New York: 2017), 421–35.

8. J. Hoberman, "Ronald Reagan's Reel Life", *NYR Daily*, June 29, 2019.

9. "The President's Past", in *Things Worth Fighting For, Collected Writings* (New York: 2004), 205.

10. Kurt Andersen, *Fantasyland: How America Went Haywire: A 500-Year History* (New York: 2017), 5.

11. Lev Manovich, *Language of New Media* (Cambridge: 2002), 270.

12. Stephen Duncombe, *Dream or Nightmare: Reimagining Politics in an Age of Fantasy* (New York: 2019), Preface.

13. Jonathan Chait, "Trump Bored by His Own Speech, Just Wants to Talk About TV Shows", *New York Magazine*, 11 Oct 2019.

14. Bob Woodward, *Fear: Trump in the White House* (New York: 2018), 88.

15. James Poniewozik, *An Audience of One: Donald Trump, Television, and the Fracturing of America* (New York: 2019), 242.

16. Tony Judt, "The Good Society: Europe vs. America", in *Reappraisals: Reflections on the Forgotten Twentieth Century* (New York: 2014), 394.

17. Ibid., 405.

18. Andersen, *Fantasyland*, 383.

19. Neil Postman, *Amusing Ourselves to Death: Public Discourse in the Age of Show Business* (New York: 2005), 116.

FIVE

1. Postman, *Amusing Ourselves to Death*, 86.

2. Cecelia Tichi, *Electronic Earth: Creating an American Television Culture* (Oxon: 1992), 39.

3. Jia Tolentino, *Trick Mirror: Reflections on Self-Delusion* (New York: 2019), 8.

4. Tom Scocca, "The Decade in Fame", *Slate*, 20 Dec 2019.

5. John Updike, *Roger's Version* (New York: 2012).

6. David Foster Wallace, "E Pluribus Unum: Television and U.S. Fiction", *Review of Contemporary Fiction* 13,2 (1993), 164.

7. See Erkki Huhtamo, "Encapsulated Bodies in Motion: Simulators and the Quest for Total Immersion", in Simon Penny (ed.), *Critical Issues in Electronic Media* (Albany: 1995), 162.

8. Poniewozick, *An Audience of One*, 240, 236.

9. Patrick Radden Keefe, "How Mark Burnett Resurrected Donald Trump as an Icon of American Success", *The New Yorker*, 27 Dec 2018.

10. Kevin O'Gorman and Andrew MacLaren, "How Donald Trump Turned the Presidency into the Greatest Reality TV Show on Earth", *The Conversation*, 23 Jan 2017.

11. See Emily Nussbaum, *I Like to Watch: Arguing My Way Through the TV Revolution* (New York: 2019).

12. Erik Hane, "The Year in Trump Novel Pitches: An Agent's Lament", *Literary Hub*, 30 Mar 2018.

13. Aleksandar Hemon, "Stop Making Sense, or How to Write in the Age of Trump", *The Village Voice*, 17 Jan 2017.

14. Matthew Yglesias, "Trump-era Politics is a Surreal Nightmare and We Can't Wake Up", *Vox*, 30 Mar 2018.

15. David Graham, "Biden's Message is Incoherent", *The Atlantic*, 12 June 2019.

16. Richard North Patterson, "I Used to Write Novels. Then Trump Rendered Fiction Redundant", *The Atlantic*, 31 Mar 2019.

17. Isaac Chotiner, "The Classicist Who Sees Donald Trump as a Classical Hero", *The New Yorker*, 20 Feb 2019.

18. "*The New York Times unites* vs. Twitter", *Slate*, 15 Aug 2019.

19. Jeet Heer, "America's First Postmodern President, *The New Republic*, 8 July 2017.

20. Andersen, *Fantasyland*, 240.

21. Eric Trump, "Hypocrisy Creates Unlevel Playing Field in Politics", *The Hill*, 3 Oct 2019.

22. Michiko Kakutani, *The Death of Truth: Notes on Falsehood in the Age of Trump* (New York: 2018).

23. Masha Gessen, "The Putin Paradigm", *NYR Daily*, 13 Dec 2016.

24. Poniewozick, *Audience of One*, 134.

25. "Plenty of Substance but Little Drama on First Day of Impeachment Hearings", *NBC News*, 13 Nov 2019.

26. Simon van Zuylen-Wood, "Pinkos Have More Fun", *New York Magazine*, 3 Mar 2019.

SIX

1. Adolf Loos, "The Poor Little Rich Man", in *Spoken into the Void: Collected Essays 1897—1900* (New York: 1987).

2. John Rawls, *Political Liberalism* (New York: 2005), 12.

3. Mark Crispin Miller, "Deride and Conquer", in Todd Gitlin (ed.), *Watching Television: A Pantheon Guide to Popular Culture*, (New York: 1986), 184.

4. James Fallows, "The End of the Roman Empire Wasn't So Bad," *The Atlantic*, October 2019.

5. John Rawls, *A Brief Enquiry Into the Meaning of Sin and Faith* (Cambridge: 2009), Introduction, 21.

6. Ibid., 266.

7. Antonio García Martínez, "How Silicon Valley Fuels an Informal Caste System," *Wired*, 7 Sep 2018.

8. Jamie Bartlett, *The People vs. Tech How the Internet Is Killing Democracy* (New York: 2018).

9. Gregory Ferenstein, "The Disrupters", *City Journal*, winter 2017.

SEVEN

1. Ron Suskind, "Faith, Certainty and the Presidency of George W. Bush", *The New York Times*, 17 Oct 2004.

2. H.G. Wells, *The Future in America: A Search After Realities* (New York: 1906), 76.

3. Reinhold Niebuhr, *The Irony of American History* (Chicago: 2008), 69.

4. Ibid., 74.

5. George F. Kennan, *Memoirs 1925–1950* (Boston: 1967), 320.

6. David Allan Mayers, *George Kennan and the Dilemmas of US Foreign Policy* (Oxon: 1990), 276.

7. Walter Hixson, "Containment on the Perimeter: George F. Kennan and Vietnam", *Diplomatic History*, 12, 2, 1988, 149–163.

8. Hans J. Morgenthau, *A New Foreign Policy for the United States* (New York: 1969), 132.

9. Leslie Gelb, *The Irony of Vietnam: The System Worked* (Washington: Brookings Institution Press, 2016), 21.

10. Ibid., 31.

11. Morgenthau, *A New Foreign Policy for the United States*, 130.

12. Henry Kissinger, *Ending the Vietnam War: A History of America's Involvement and Extrication from the Vietnam War* (New York: 2003), 13

13. Ibid., 556–560.

14. Walter Hixson, *George F. Kennan: Cold War Iconoclast* (New York: 1989), 236.

15. Garry Wills, *Reagan's America: Innocents at Home* (New York: 1986), 2–3.

16. Michael Mann, *States, War and Capitalism: Studies in Political Sociology* (Oxon: 1988), 185.

17. Andrew J. Bacevich, *The New American Militarism, How Americans Are Seduced by War* (Oxon: 2005), 115.

18. Lawrence Freedman, Introduction, The Adelphi Papers, 38,318, *The Revolution in Strategic Affairs*, 29.

19. James William Gibson, *The Perfect War: The* War *We Couldn't Lose and How We Did* (New York: 1988), 364.

20. Phil Stanford, "The Automated Battlefield", *The New York Times Magazine*, 23 Feb. 1975.

21. Keith L. Shimko, *The Iraq Wars and America's Military Revolution* (Cambridge: 2010), 40, 57.

22. Jean Baudrillard, *The Gulf War Did Not Take Place* (Bloomington: 1995), 31.

23. Frank Rich, "The Age of the Mediathon", *The New York Times*, 29 Oct 2000.

24. President Bill Clinton, remarks to the Kosovo Force (KFOR) troops, Skopje, Macedonia, 22 June 1999.

25. Michael Ignatieff, *Virtual War: Kosovo and Beyond* (London: 2000), 3, 142–3, 214–15.

26. Henry Kissinger, *Does America Need a Foreign Policy? Towards a Diplomacy for the 21st Century* (New York: 2001), 257.

27. Ahsan I. Butt, "Why Did the United States Invade Iraq in 2003?", *Security Studies*, 28,2 (2019), 35.

28. See Bruno Maçães, *The Dawn of Eurasia*.

29. Brooks Adams, "Russia's Interest in China", in *America's Economic Supremacy* (New York: 2000), 221.

30. See Bruno Maçães, *Belt and Road: A Chinese World Order* (London: 2018).

31. Address delivered by President Roosevelt at Charlottesville, Virginia, 10 June 1940.

32. See Mikhail Bakhtin, *Problems of Dostoevsky's Poetics* (Minneapolis: 1984).

33. "The U.S., China, and Pluralism in International Affairs", Brookings Institution, 2 Dec 2019.

INDEX

INDEX

INDEX

INDEX

INDEX

INDEX

INDEX

INDEX

INDEX

INDEX

INDEX

INDEX

INDEX

INDEX

INDEX